Misalliance

A DEBATE IN ONE SITTING

By George Bernard Shaw

SAMUEL FRENCH, INC.

45 WEST 25TH STREET	NEW YORK 10010
7623 SUNSET BOULEVARD	HOLLYWOOD 90046
LONDON	*TORONTO*

Misalliance

with
A Treatise on Parents and Children
Silent Audiences
The Repertory Theatre
Author's Note

Composition begun 8 September 1909; completed 4 November 1909. First published in German translation, as *Mesallianz*, 1910. Published in *Misalliance, The Dark Lady of the Sonnets,* and *Fanny's First Play,* 1914. Revised text in Collected Edition, 1930. First presented at the Duke of York's Theatre, London, on 23 February 1910.

JOHN TARLETON, JUN.	*Frederick Lloyd*
BENTLEY SUMMERHAYS	*Donald Calthrop*
HYPATIA TARLETON	*Miriam Lewes*
MRS. TARLETON	*Florence Haydon*
LORD SUMMERHAYS	*Hubert Harben*
JOHN TARLETON	*C. M. Lowne*
JOSEPH PERCIVAL	*Charles Bryant*
LINA SZCZEPANOWSKA	*Lena Ashwell*
JULIUS BAKER ("GUNNER")	*O. P. Heggie*

PERIOD: 31 May 1909

SCENE: The House of John Tarleton, of Hindhead, Surrey

"As the debate is a long one (the play was originally sub-titled 'A Debate in One Sitting'), the curtain will be lowered twice. The audience is requested to excuse these interruptions, which are made solely for its convenience."

Parents and Children

CONTENTS

5

6　　MISALLIANCE

TRAILING CLOUDS OF GLORY

Childhood is a stage in the process of that continual re-manufacture of the Life Stuff by which the human race is perpetuated. The Life Force either will not or cannot achieve immortality except in very low organisms: indeed it is by no means ascertained that even the amoeba is immortal. Human beings visibly wear out, though they last longer than their friends the dogs. Turtles, parrots, and elephants are believed to be capable of outliving the memory of the oldest human inhabitant. But the fact that new ones are born conclusively proves that they are not immortal. Do away with death and you do away with the need for birth: in fact if you went on breeding, you would finally have to kill old people to make room for young ones.

Now death is not necessarily a failure of energy on the part of the Life Force. People with no imagination try to make things which will last for ever, and even want to live for ever themselves. But the intelligently imaginative man knows very well that it is waste of labor to make machine that will last ten years, because it will probably be superseded in half that time by an improved machine answering the same purpose. He also knows that if some devil were to convince us that our dream of personal immortality is no dream but a hard fact, such a shriek of despair would go up from the human race as no other conceivable horror could provoke. With all our perverse nonsense as to John Smith living for a thousand million eons and for ever after, we die voluntarily, knowing that it is time for us to be scrapped, to be remanufactured, to come back, as Wordsworth divined, trailing ever brightening clouds of glory. We must all be born again, and yet again and again. We should like to live a little longer just as we should like £50: that is, we should take it if we could get it for nothing; but that sort of idle liking is not will. It is amazing—considering the way we talk—how little a man will do to get £50: all the £50 notes I have ever known of have been more easily earned than a laborious sixpence; but the difficulty of inducing a man to make any serious effort to obtain £50 is nothing to the difficulty of inducing him to make a serious effort to keep alive. The moment he sees death approach, he gets into bed and sends for a doctor. He knows very well at the back of his conscience that he is rather a poor job and had better be remanufactured. He knows that his death will make room for a birth; and he hopes that it will be a birth of something that he aspired to be and fell short of. He knows that it is through death and rebirth that this corruptible shall become incorruptible, and this mortal put on immortality. Practise as you will on his ignorance, his fears, and his imagination with bribes of paradises and threats of hells, there is only one belief that can rob death of its sting and the grave of its victory; and that is the belief that we can lay down the burden of our wretched little makeshift individualities for ever at each lift towards the goal of evolution, which can only be a being that cannot be improved upon. After all, what man is capable of the insane self-conceit of believing that an eternity of himself would be tolerable even to himself? Those who try to believe it postulate that they shall be made perfect first. But if you make me perfect I shall no longer be myself, nor will it be possible for me to conceive my present imperfections (and what I cannot conceive I cannot remember); so that you may just as well give me a new name and face the fact that I am a new person and that the old Bernard Shaw is as dead as mutton. Thus, oddly enough, the conventional belief in the matter comes to this: that if you wish to live for ever you must be wicked enough to be irretrievably damned, since the saved are no longer what they were, and in hell alone do people retain their sinful nature: that is to say, their individuality. And this sort of hell, however convenient as a means of intimidating persons who have practically no honor and no conscience, is not a fact. Death is for many of us the gate of hell; but we are inside on the way out, not outside on the way in. Therefore let us give up telling one another idle stories, and rejoice in death as we rejoice in birth; for without death we cannot be born again; and the man who does not wish to be born again and born better is fit only to represent the City of London in Parliament, or perhaps the university of Oxford.

THE CHILD IS FATHER TO THE MAN

Is he? Then in the name of common sense why do we always treat children on the assumption that the man is father to the child? Oh, these fathers! And we are not content with fathers: we must have godfathers, forgetting that the child is godfather to the man. Has it ever struck you as curious that in a country where the first article of belief is that every child is born with a godfather whom we all call "our father which art in heaven," two very limited individual mortals should be allowed to appear at its baptism and explain that they are its godparents, and that they will look after its salvation until it is no longer a child. I had a godmother who made herself responsible in this way for me. She presented me with a Bible with a gilt clasp and edges, larger than the Bibles similarly presented to my sisters, because my sex entitled me to a heavier article. I must have seen that lady at least four times in the twenty years following. She never alluded to my salvation in any way. People occasionally ask me to act as godfather to their children with a levity which convinces me that they have not the faintest notion that it involves anything more than calling the helpless child George Bernard without regard to the possibility that it may grow up in the liveliest abhorrence of my notions.

A person with a turn for logic might argue that if God is the Father of all men, and if the child is father to the man, it follows that the true representative of God at the christening is the child itself. But such posers are unpopular, because they imply that our little customs, or, as we often call them, our religion, mean something, or must originally have meant something, and that we understand and believe that something.

However, my business is not to make confusion worse confounded, but to clear it up. Only, it is as well to begin by a sample of current thought and practice which shews that on the subject of children we are very deeply confused. On the whole, whatever our theory or no theory may be, our practice is is to treat the child as the property of its immediate physical parents, and to allow them to do what they like with it as far as it will let them. It has no rights and no liberties: in short, its condition is that which adults recognize as the most miserable and dangerous politically possible for themselves: namely, the condition of slavery. For its alleviation we trust to the natural affection of the parties, and to public opinion. A father cannot for his own credit let his son go in rags. Also, in a very large section of the population, parents finally become dependent on their children. Thus there are checks on child slavery which do not exist, or are less powerful, in the case of manual and industrial slavery. Sensationally bad cases fall into two classes, which are really the same class: namely, the children whose parents are excessively addicted to the sensual luxury of petting children, and the children whose parents are excessively addicted to the sensual luxury of physically torturing them. There is a Society for the Prevention of Cruelty to Children which has effectually made an end of our belief that mothers are any more to be trusted than stepmothers, or fathers than slave-drivers. And there is a growing body of law designed to prevent parents from using their children ruthlessly to make money for the household. Such legislation has always been furiously resisted by the parents, even when the horrors of factory slavery were at their worst; and the extension of such legislation at present would be impossible if it were not that the parents affected by it cannot control a majority of votes in Parliament. In domestic life a great deal of service is done by children, the girls acting as nursemaids and general servants, and the lads as errand boys. In the country both boys and girls do a substantial share of farm labor. This is why it is necessary to coerce poor parents to send their children to school, though in the relatively small class which keeps plenty of servants it is impossible to induce parents to keep their children at home instead of paying schoolmasters to take them off their hands.

It appears then that the bond of affection between parents and children does not save children from the slavery that denial of rights involves in adult political relations. It sometimes intensifies it, sometimes mitigates it; but on the whole children and parents confront one another as two classes in which all the political power is on one side; and the results are not at all unlike what they would be if there were no immediate consanguinity between them, and one were white and the other black, or one enfranchised and the other disenfranchised, or one ranked as gentle and the other simple. Not that Nature counts for nothing in the case and political rights for everything. But a denial of political rights, and the resultant delivery of one class into the mastery of another, affects their relations so extensively and profoundly that it is impossible to ascertain what the real natural relations of the two classes are until this political relation is abolished.

WHAT IS A CHILD?

An experiment. A fresh attempt to produce the just man made perfect: that is, to make humanity divine. And you will vitiate the experiment if you make the slightest attempt to abort it into some fancy figure of your own: for example, your notion of a good man or a womanly woman. If you treat it as a little wild beast to be tamed, or as a pet to be played with, or even as a means to save you trouble and to make money for you (and these are our commonest ways), it may fight its way through in spite of you and save its soul alive; for all its instincts will resist you, and possibly be strengthened in the resistance;

but if you begin with its own holiest aspirations, and suborn them for your own purposes, then there is hardly any limit to the mischief you may do. Swear at a child, throw your boots at it, send it flying from the room with a cuff or a kick; and the experience will be as instructive to the child as a difficulty with a short-tempered dog or a bull. Francis Place tells us that his father always struck his children when he found one within his reach. The effect on the young Places seems to have been simply to make them keep out of their father's way, which was no doubt what he desired, as far as he desired anything at all. Francis records the habit without bitterness, having reason to thank his stars that his father respected the inside of his head whilst cuffing the outside of it; and this made it easy for Francis to do yeoman's service to his country as that rare and admirable thing, a Freethinker: the only sort of thinker, I may remark, whose thoughts, and consequently whose religious convictions, command any respect.

Now Mr Place, senior, would be described by many as a bad father; and I do not contend that he was a conspicuously good one. But as compared with the conventional good father who deliberately imposes himself on his son as a god; who takes advantage of childish credulity and parent worship to persuade his son that what he approves of is right and what he disapproves of is wrong; who imposes a corresponding conduct on the child by a system of prohibitions and penalties, rewards and eulogies, for which he claims divine sanction: compared to this sort of abortionist and monster maker, I say, Place appears almost as a Providence. Not that it is possible to live with children any more than with grown-up people without imposing rules of conduct on them. There is a point at which every person with human nerves has to say to a child "Stop that noise." But suppose the child asks why! There are various answers in use. The simplest: "Because it irritates me," may fail; for it may strike the child as being rather amusing to irritate you; also the child, having comparatively no nerves, may be unable to conceive your meaning vividly enough. In any case it may want to make a noise more than to spare your feelings. You may therefore have to explain that the effect of the irritation will be that you will do something unpleasant if the noise continues. The something unpleasant may be only a look of suffering to rouse the child's affectionate sympathy (if it has any), or it may run to forcible expulsion from the room with plenty of unnecessary violence; but the principle is the same: there are no false pretences involved: the child learns in a straightforward way that it does not pay to be inconsiderate. Also, perhaps, that Mamma, who made the child learn the Sermon on the Mount, is not really a Christian.

THE SIN OF NADAB AND ABIHU

But there is another sort of answer in wide use which is neither straightforward, instructive, nor harmless. In its simplest form it substitutes for "Stop that noise," "Dont be naughty," which means that the child, instead of annoying you by a perfectly healthy and natural infantile procedure, is offending God. This is a blasphemous lie; and the fact that it is on the lips of every nurserymaid does not excuse it in the least. Dickens tells us of a nurserymaid who elaborated it into "If you do that, angels wont never love you." I remember a servant who used to tell me that if I were not good, by which she meant if I did not behave with a single eye to her personal convenience, the cock would come down the chimney. Less imaginative but equally dishonest people told me I should go to hell if I did not make myself agreeable to them. Bodily violence, provided it be the hasty expression of normal provoked resentment and not vicious cruelty, cannot harm a child as this sort of pious fraud harms it. There is a legal limit to physical cruelty; and there are also human limits to it. There is an active Society which brings to book a good many parents who starve and torture and overwork their children, and intimidates a good many more. When parents of this type are caught, they are treated as criminals; and not infrequently the police have some trouble to save them from being lynched. The people against whom children are wholly unprotected are those who devote themselves to the very mischievous and cruel sort of abortion which is called bringing up a child in the way it should go. Now nobody knows the way a child should go. All the ways discovered so far lead to the horrors of our existing civilizations, described quite justifiably by Ruskin as heaps of agonizing human maggots, struggling with one another for scraps of food. Pious fraud is an attempt to pervert that divine mystery called the child's conscience into an instrument of our own convenience, and to use that wonderful and terrible power called Shame to grind our own axe. It is the sin of stealing fire from the altar: a sin so impudently practised by popes, parents, and pedagogues, that one can hardly expect the nurserymaids to see any harm in stealing a few cinders when they are worried.

Into the blackest depths of this violation of children's souls one can hardly bear to look; for here we find pious fraud masking the violation of the body by obscene cruelty. Any parent or school teacher who takes a secret and abominable delight in torture is allowed to lay traps into which every child must fall, and then beat it to his or her heart's content. A gentleman once wrote to me and said, with an obvious conviction that he was being most reasonable and high-minded, that the only thing he beat his children for was failure in perfect obedience and perfect truthfulness. On these virtues, he said, he must insist. As one of them is not a virtue at all, and the other is the attribute of a god, one can imagine what the lives of this gentleman's children would have been if it had been possible for him to live down to his monstrous and foolish pretensions. And yet he might have written his letter to The Times (he very nearly did, by the way) without incurring any danger of being removed to a asylum, or even losing his reputation for taking a very proper view of his parental duties. And at least it was not a trivial view, nor an ill meant one. It was much more respectable than the general consensus of opinion that if a school teacher can devise a question a child cannot answer, or overhear it calling omega omeega, he or she may beat the child viciously. Only, the cruelty must be whitewashed by a moral excuse, and a pretence of reluctance. It must be for the child's good. The assailant must say "This hurts me more than it hurts you." There must be hypocrisy as well as cruelty. The injury to the child would be far less if the voluptuary said frankly "I beat you because I like beating you; and I shall do it whenever I can contrive an excuse for it." But to represent this detestable lust to the child as Divine wrath, and the cruelty as the beneficent act of God, which is exactly what all our floggers do, is to add to the torture of the body, out of which the flogger at least gets some pleasure, the maiming and blinding of the child's soul, which can bring nothing but horror to anyone.

THE MANUFACTURE OF MONSTERS

This industry is by no means peculiar to China. The Chinese (they say) make physical monsters. We revile them for it and proceed to make moral monsters of our own children. The most excusable parents are those who try to correct their own faults in their offspring. The parent who says to his child: "I am one of the successes of the Almighty: therefore imitate me in every particular or I will have the skin off your back" (a quite common attitude) is a much more absurd figure than the man who, with a pipe in his mouth, thrashes his boy for smoking. If you must hold yourself up to your children as an object lesson (which is not at all necessary), hold yourself up as a warning and not as an example. But you had much better let the child's character alone. If you once allow yourself to regard a child as so much material for you to manufacture into any shape that happens to suit your fancy you are defeating the experiment of the Life Force. You are assuming that the child does not know its own business, and that you do. In this you are sure to be wrong: the child feels the drive of the Life Force (often called the Will of God); and you cannot feel it for him. Handel's parents no doubt thought they knew better than their child when they tried to prevent his becoming a musician. They would have been equally wrong and equally unsuccessful if they had tried to prevent the child becoming a great rascal had its genius lain in that direction. Handel would have been Handel, and Napoleon and Peter of Russia *them*selves in spite of all the parents in creation, because, as often happens, they were stronger than their parents. But this does not happen always. Most children can be, and many are, hopelessly warped and wasted by parents who are ignorant and silly enough to suppose that they know what a human being ought to be, and who stick at nothing in their determination to force their children into their moulds. Every child has a right to its own bent. It has a right to be a Plymouth Brother though its parents be convinced atheists. It has a right to dislike its mother or father or sister or brother or uncle or aunt if they are antipathetic to it. It has a right to find its own way and go its own way, whether that way seems wise or foolish to others, exactly as an adult has. It has a right to privacy as to its own doings and its own affairs as much as if it were its own father.

SMALL AND LARGE FAMILIES

These rights have now become more important than they used to be, because the modern practice of limiting families enables them to be more effectually violated. In a family of ten, eight, six, or even four children, the rights of the younger ones to a great extent take care of themselves and of the rights of the elder ones too. Two adult parents, in spite of a house to keep and an income to earn, can still interfere to a disastrous extent with the rights and liberties of one child. But by the time a fourth child has arrived, they are not only outnumbered two to one, but are getting tired of the thankless and mischievous job of bringing up their children in the way they think they should go. The old observation that members of large families get on in the world holds good because in large families it is impossible for each child to receive what schoolmasters call "individual attention." The children may receive a good deal of individual attention from one another in the shape of outspoken reproach, ruthless ridicule, and violent resistance to their attempts at aggression; but the parental despots are compelled by the multitude of their subjects to resort to political rather than personal rule, and to spread their attempts at moral monster-making over so many children, that each child has enough freedom, and enough sport in the prophylactic process of laughing at its elders behind their backs, to escape with much less damage than the single child. In a large school the system may be bad; but the personal influence of the head master has to be exerted, when it is exerted at all, in a public way, because he has little more power of working on the affections of the individual scholar in the intimate way that, for example, the mother of a single child can, than the prime minister has of working on the affections of any individual voter.

CHILDREN AS NUISANCES

Experienced parents, when children's rights are preached to them, very naturally ask whether children are to be allowed to do what they like. The best reply is to ask whether adults are to be allowed to do what they like. The two cases are the same. The adult who is nasty is not allowed to do what he likes: neither can the child who likes to be nasty. There is no difference in principle between the rights of a child and those of an adult: the difference in their cases is one of circumstance. An adult is not supposed to be punished except by process of law; nor, when he is so punished, is the person whom he has injured allowed to act as judge, jury, and executioner. It is true that employers do act in this way every day to their workpeople; but this is not a justified and intended part of the situation: it is an abuse of Capitalism which nobody defends in principle. As between child and parent or nurse it is not argued about because it is inevitable. You cannot hold an impartial judicial inquiry every time a child misbehaves itself. To allow the child to misbehave without instantly making it unpleasantly conscious of the fact would be to spoil it. The adult has therefore to take some action of some sort with nothing but his conscience to shield the child from injustice or unkindness. The action may be a torrent of scolding culminating in a furious smack causing terror and pain, or it may be a remonstrance causing remorse, or it may be a sarcasm causing shame and humiliation, or it may be a sermon causing the child to believe that it is a little reprobate on the road to hell. The child has no defence in any case except the kindness and conscience of the adult; and the adult had better not forget this; for it involves a heavy responsibility.

And now comes our difficulty. The responsibility, being so heavy, cannot be discharged by persons of feeble character or intelligence. And yet people of high character and intelligence cannot be plagued with the care of children. A child is a restless, noisy little animal, with an insatiable appetite for knowledge, and consequently a maddening persistence in asking questions. If the child is to remain in the room with a highly intelligent and sensitive adult, it must be told, and if necessary forced, to sit still and not speak, which is injurious to its health, unnatural, unjust, and therefore cruel and selfish beyond toleration. Consequently the highly intelligent and sensitive adult hands the child over to a nurserymaid who has no nerves and can therefore stand more noise, but who has also no scruples, and may therefore be very bad company for the child.

Here we have come to the central fact of the question: a fact nobody avows, which is yet the true explanation of the monstrous system of child imprisonment and torture which we disguise under such hypocrisies as education, training, formation of character and the rest of it. This fact is simply that a child is a nuisance to a grown-up person. What is more, the nuisance becomes more and more intolerable as the grown-up person becomes more cultivated, more sensitive, and more deeply engaged in the highest methods of adult work. The child at play is noisy and ought to be noisy: Sir Isaac Newton at work is quiet and ought to be quiet. And the child should spend most of its time at play, whilst the adult should spend most of his time at work. I am not now writing on behalf of persons who coddle themselves into a ridiculous condition of nervous feebleness, and at last imagine themselves unable to work under conditions of bustle which to healthy people are cheerful and stimulating. I am sure that if people had to choose between living where the noise of children never stopped and where it was never heard, all the goodnatured and sound people would prefer the incessant noise to the incessant silence. But that choice is not thrust upon us by the nature of things. There is no reason why children and adults should not see just as much of one another as is good for them, no more and no less. Even at present you are not compelled to choose between sending your child to a boarding school (which means getting rid of it altogether on more or less hypocritical pretences) and keeping it continually at home. Most working folk today either send their children to day schools or turn them out of doors. This solves the problem for the parents. It does not solve it for the children, any more than the tethering of a goat in a field or the chasing of an unlicensed dog into the streets solves it for the goat or the dog; but it shews that in no class are people willing to endure the society of their children, and

consequently that it is an error to believe that the family
provides children with edifying adult society, or that the
family is a social unit. The family is in that, as in so
many other respects, a humbug. Old people and young
people cannot walk at the same pace without distress and
final loss of health to one of the parties. When they are
sitting indoors they cannot endure the same degrees of
temperature and the same supplies of fresh air. Even if
the main factors of noise, restlessness, and inquisitiveness
are left out of account, children can stand with indifference sights, sounds, smells, and disorders that would make
an adult of fifty utterly miserable; whilst on the other
hand such adults find a tranquil happiness in conditions
which to children mean unspeakable boredom. And since
our system is nevertheless to pack them all into the same
house and pretend that they are happy, and that this
particular sort of happiness is the foundation of virtue, it
is found that in discussing family life we never speak of
actual adults or actual children, or of realities of any sort,
but always of ideals such as The Home, a Mother's Influence, a Father's Care, Filial Piety, Duty, Affection,
Family Life, etc. etc., which are no doubt very comforting phrases, but which beg the question of what a home
and a mother's influence and a father's care and so forth
really come to in practice. How many hours a week of
the time when his children are out of bed does the ordinary breadwinning father spend in the company of his
children or even in the same building with them? The
home may be a thieves' kitchen, the mother a procuress,
the father a violent drunkard; or the mother and father
may be fashionable people who see their children three
or four times a year during the holidays, and then not
oftener than they can help, living meanwhile in daily and
intimate contact with their valets and lady's-maids, whose
influence and care are often dominant in the household.
Affection, as distinguished from simple kindliness, may
or may not exist: when it does it either depends on
qualities in the parties that would produce it equally if

they were of no kin to one another, or it is a more or less morbid survival of the nursing passion; for affection between adults (if they are really adult in mind and not merely grownup children) and creatures so relatively selfish and cruel as children necessarily are without knowing it or meaning it, cannot be called natural: in fact the evidence shews that it is easier to love the company of a dog than of a commonplace child between the ages of six and the beginnings of controlled maturity; for women who cannot bear to be separated from their pet dogs send their children to boarding schools cheerfully. They may say and even believe that in allowing their children to leave home they are sacrificing themselves for their children's good; but there are very few pet dogs who would not be the better for a month or two spent elsewhere than in a lady's lap or roasting on a drawing-room hearthrug. Besides, to allege that children are better continually away from home is to give up the whole popular sentimental theory of the family; yet the dogs are kept and the children are banished.

CHILD FANCIERS

There is, however, a good deal of spurious family affection. There is the clannishness that will make a dozen brothers and sisters who quarrel furiously among themselves close up their ranks and make common cause against a brother-in-law or a sister-in-law. And there is a strong sense of property in children, which often makes mothers and fathers bitterly jealous of allowing anyone else to interfere with their children, whom they may none the less treat very badly. And there is an extremely dangerous craze for children which leads certain people to establish orphanages and baby farms and schools, seizing any pretext for filling their houses with children exactly as some eccentric old ladies and gentlemen fill theirs with cats. In such places the children are the victims of all the caprices of doting affection and all the excesses of lascivious cruelty. Yet the people who have this morbid craze seldom have any difficulty in finding victims. Parents and guardians are so worried by children and so anxious to get rid of them that anyone who is willing to take them off their hands is welcomed and whitewashed. The very people who read with indignation of Squeers and Creakle in the novels of Dickens are quite ready to hand over their own children to Squeers and Creakle, and to pretend that Squeers and Creakle are monsters of the past. But read the autobiography of Stanley the traveller, or sit in the company of men talking about their schooldays, and you will soon find that fiction, which must, if it is to be sold and read, stop short of being positively sickening, dare not tell the whole truth about the people to whom children are handed over on educational pretexts. Not very long ago a schoolmaster in Ireland was murdered by his boys; and for reasons which were never made public it was at first decided not to prosecute the murderers. Yet all these flogging schoolmasters and orphanage fiends and baby farmers are "lovers of children." They are really child fanciers (like bird fanciers or dog fanciers) by irresistible natural predilection, never happy unless they are surrounded by their victims, and always certain to make their living by accepting custody of children, no matter how many alternative occupations may be available. And bear in mind that they are only the extreme instances of what is commonly called natural affection, apparently because it is obviously unnatural.

The really natural feeling of adults for children in the long prosaic intervals between the moments of affectionate impulse is just that feeling that leads them to avoid their care and constant company as a burden beyond bearing, and to pretend that the places they send them to are well conducted, beneficial, and indispensable to the success of the children in after life. The true cry of the kind mother after her little rosary of kisses is "Run away, darling." It is nicer than "Hold your noise, you young devil; or it will be the worse for you;" but fundamentally it means the same thing: that if you compel an adult and a child to live in one another's company either the adult or the child will be miserable. There is nothing whatever unnatural or wrong or shocking in this fact; and there is no harm in it if only it be sensibly faced and provided for. The mischief that it does at present is produced by our efforts to ignore it, or to smother it under a heap of sentimental lies and false pretences.

CHILDHOOD AS A STATE OF SIN

Unfortunately all this nonsense tends to accumulate as we become more sympathetic. In many families it is still the custom to treat childhood frankly as a state of sin, and impudently proclaim the monstrous principle that little children should be seen and not heard, and to enforce a set of prison rules designed solely to make cohabitation with children as convenient as possible for adults without the smallest regard for the interests, either remote or immediate, of the children. This system tends to produce a tough, rather brutal, stupid, unscrupulous class, with a fixed idea that all enjoyment consists in undetected sinning; and in certain phases of civilization people of this kind are apt to get the upper hand of more amiable and conscientious races and classes. They have the ferocity of a chained dog, and are proud of it. But the end of it is that they are always in chains, even at the height of their military or political success; they win everything on condition that they are afraid to enjoy it. Their civilizations rest on intimidation, which is so necessary to them that when they cannot find anybody brave enough to intimidate them they intimidate themselves and live in a continual moral and political panic. In the end they get found out and bullied. But that is not the point that concerns us here, which is, that they are in some respects better brought up than the children of sentimental people who are always anxious and miserable about their duty to their children, and who end by neither making their children happy nor having a tolerable life for themselves. A selfish tyrant you know where to have, and he (or she) at least does not confuse your affections; but a conscientious and kindly meddler may literally worry you out of your senses. It is fortunate that only very few parents are capable of doing what they conceive their duty continually or even at all, and that still fewer are tough enough to ride roughshod over their children at home.

SCHOOL

But please observe the limitation "at home." What private amateur parental enterprise cannot do may be done very effectively by organized professional enterprise in large institutions established for the purpose. And it is to such professional enterprise that parents hand over their children when they can afford it. They send their children to school; and there is, on the whole, nothing on earth intended for innocent people so horrible as a school. To begin with, it is a prison. But it is in some respects more cruel than a prison. In a prison, for instance, you are not forced to read books written by the warders and the governor (who of course would not be warders and governors if they could write readable books), and beaten or otherwise tormented if you cannot remember their utterly unmemorable contents. In the prison you are not forced to sit listening to turnkeys discoursing without charm or interest on subjects that they dont understand and dont care about, and are therefore incapable of making you understand or care about. In a prison they may torture your body; but they do not torture your brains; and they protect you against violence and outrage from your fellow-prisoners. In a school you have none of these advantages. With the world's bookshelves loaded with fascinating and inspired books, the very manna sent down from Heaven to feed your souls, you are forced to read a hideous imposture called a school book, written by a man who cannot write: a book from which no human being can learn anything: a book which, though you may decipher it, you cannot in any fruitful sense read, though the enforced attempt will make you loathe the sight of a book all the rest of your life. With millions of acres of woods and valleys and hills and wind and air and birds and streams and fishes and all sorts of instructive and healthy things easily accessible, or with streets and shop windows and crowds and vehicles and all sorts of city delights at the door, you are forced to sit, not in a room with some human grace and comfort of furniture and decoration, but in a stalled pound with a lot of other children, beaten if you talk, beaten if you move, beaten if you cannot prove by answering idiotic questions that even when you escaped from the pound and from the eye of your gaoler, you were still agonizing over his detestable sham books instead of daring to live. And your childish hatred of your gaoler and flogger is nothing to his adult hatred of you; for he is a slave forced to endure your society for his daily bread. You have not even the satisfaction of knowing how you are torturing him and how he loathes you; and you give yourself unnecessary pains to annoy him with furtive tricks and spiteful doing of forbidden things. No wonder he is sometimes provoked to fiendish outbursts of wrath. No wonder men of downright sense, like Dr Johnson, admit that under such circumstances children will not learn anything unless they are so cruelly beaten that they make desperate efforts to memorize words and phrases to escape flagellation. It is a ghastly business, quite beyond words, this schooling.

And now I hear cries of protest arising all round. First my own schoolmasters, or their ghosts, asking whether I was cruelly beaten at school? No; but then I did not learn anything at school. Dr Johnson's schoolmaster presumably did care enough whether Sam learned anything to beat him savagely enough to force him to lame his mind—for Johnson's great mind *was* lamed—by learning his lessons.

None of my schoolmasters really cared a rap (or perhaps it would be fairer to them to say that their employers did not care a rap and therefore did not give them the necessary caning powers) whether I learnt my lessons or not, provided my father paid my schooling bill, the collection of which was the real object of the school. Consequently I did not learn my school lessons, having much more important ones in hand, with the result that I have not wasted my life trifling with literary fools in taverns as Johnson did when he should have been shaking England with the thunder of his spirit. My schooling did me a great deal of harm and no good whatever: it was simply dragging a child's soul through the dirt; but I escaped Squeers and Creakle just as I escaped Johnson and Carlyle. And this is what happens to most of us. We are not effectively coerced to learn: we stave off punishment as far as we can by lying and trickery and guessing and using our wits; and when this does not suffice we scribble impositions, or suffer extra imprisonments— "keeping in" was the phrase in my time—or let a master strike us with a cane and fall back on our pride at being able to bear it physically (he not being allowed to hit us too hard) to outface the dishonor we should have been taught to die rather than endure. And so idleness and worthlessness on the one hand and a pretence of coercion on the other became a despicable routine. If my schoolmasters had been really engaged in educating me instead of painfully earning their bread by keeping me from annoying my elders they would have turned me out of the school, telling me that I was thoroughly disloyal to it; that I had no intention of learning; that I was mocking and distracting the boys who did wish to learn; that I was a liar and a shirker and a seditious little nuisance; and that nothing could injure me in character and degrade their occupation more than allowing me (much less forcing me) to remain in the school under such conditions. But in order to get expelled, it was necessary to commit a crime of such atrocity that the parents of the other boys would have threatened to remove their sons sooner than allow them to be schoolfellows with the delinquent. I can remember only one case in which such a penalty was threatened; and in that case the culprit, a boarder, had kissed a housemaid, or possibly, being a handsome youth, been kissed by her. She did not kiss me; and nobody ever dreamt of expelling me. The truth was, a boy meant just so much a year to the institution. That was why he was kept there against his will. That was why he was kept there when his expulsion would have been an unspeakable relief and benefit both to his teachers and himself.

It may be argued that if the uncommercial attitude had been taken, and all the disloyal wasters and idlers shewn sternly to the door, the school would not have been emptied, but filled. But so honest an attitude was impossible. The masters must have hated the school much more than the boys did. Just as you cannot imprison a man without imprisoning a warder to see that he does not escape, the warder being tied to the prison as effectually by the fear of unemployment and starvation as the prisoner is by the bolts and bars, so these poor schoolmasters, with their small salaries and large classes, were as much prisoners as we were, and much more responsible and anxious ones. They could not impose the heroic attitude on their employers; nor would they have been able to obtain places as schoolmasters if their habits had been heroic. For the best of them their employment was provisional: they looked forward to escaping from it into the pulpit. The ablest and most impatient of them were often so irritated by the awkward, slow-witted, slovenly boys: that is, the ones that required special consideration and patient treatment, that they vented their irritation on them ruthlessly, nothing being easier than to entrap or bewilder such a boy into giving a pretext for punishing him.

MY SCHOLASTIC ACQUIREMENTS

The results, as far as I was concerned, were what might have been expected. My school made only the thinnest pretence of teaching anything but Latin and Greek. When I went there as a very small boy I knew a good deal of Latin grammar which I had been taught in a few weeks privately by my uncle. When I had been several years at school this same uncle examined me and discovered that the net result of my schooling was that I had forgotten what he had taught me, and had learnt nothing else. To this day, though I can still decline a Latin noun and repeat some of the old paradigms in the old meaningless way, because their rhythm sticks to me, I have never yet seen a Latin inscription on a tomb that I could translate throughout. Of Greek I can decipher perhaps the greater part of the Greek alphabet. In short, I am, as to classical education, another Shakespear. I can read French as easily as English; and under pressure of necessity I can turn to account some scraps of German and a little operatic Italian; but these I was never taught at school. Instead, I was taught lying, dishonorable submission to tyranny, dirty stories, a blasphemous habit of treating love and maternity as obscene jokes, hopelessness, evasion, derision, cowardice, and all the blackguard's shifts by which the coward intimidates other cowards. And if I had been a boarder at an English public school instead of a day boy at an Irish one, I might have had to add to these, deeper shames still.

SCHOOLMASTERS OF GENIUS

And now, if I have reduced the ghosts of my schoolmasters to melancholy acquiescence in all this (which everybody who has been at an ordinary school will recognize as true), I have still to meet the much more sincere protests of the handful of people who have a natural genius for "bringing up" children. I shall be asked with kindly scorn whether I have heard of Froebel and Pestalozzi, whether I know the work that is being done by Miss Mason and the Dottoressa Montessori or, best of all as I think, the Eurythmics School of Jacques Dalcroze at Hellerau near Dresden. Jacques Dalcroze, like Plato, believes in saturating his pupils with music. They walk to music, play to music, work to music, obey drill commands that would bewilder a guardsman to music, think to music, live to music, get so clearheaded about music that they can move their several limbs each in a different metre until they become complicated living magazines of cross rhythms, and, what is more, make music for others to do all these things to. Stranger still, though Jacques Dalcroze, like all these great teachers, is the completest of tyrants, knowing what is right and that he must and will have the lesson just so or else break his heart (not somebody else's, observe), yet his school is so fascinating that every woman who sees it exclaims "Oh, why was I not taught like this!" and elderly gentlemen excitedly enrol themselves as students and distract classes of infants by their desperate endeavors to beat two in a bar with one hand and three with the other, and start off on earnest walks round the room, taking two steps backward whenever Monsieur Dalcroze calls out "Hop!" Oh yes: I know all about these wonderful schools that you cannot keep children or even adults out of, and these teachers whom their pupils not only obey without coercion, but adore. And if you will tell me roughly how many Masons and Montessoris and Dalcrozes you think you can pick up in Europe for salaries of from thirty shillings to five pounds a week, I will estimate your chances of converting your millions of little scholastic hells into little scholastic heavens. If you are a distressed gentlewoman starting to make a living, you can still open a little school: and you can easily buy a secondhand brass plate inscribed PESTALOZZIAN INSTITUTE and nail it to your door, though you have no more idea of who Pestalozzi was and what he advocated or how he did it than the manager of a hotel which began as a Hydropathic has of the water cure. Or you can buy a cheaper plate inscribed KINDERGARTEN, and imagine, or leave others to imagine, that Froebel is the governing genius of your little *crèche*. No doubt the new brass plates are being inscribed Montessori Institute, and will be used when the Dottoressa is no longer with us by all the Mrs Pipchins and Mrs Wilfers throughout this unhappy land.

I will go further, and admit that the brass plates may not all be frauds. I will tell you that one of my friends was led to genuine love and considerable knowledge of classical literature by an Irish schoolmaster whom you would call a hedge schoolmaster (he would not be allowed to teach anything now) and that it took four years of Harrow to obliterate that knowledge and change the love into loathing. Another friend of mine who keeps a school in the suburbs, and who deeply deplores my "prejudice against schoolmasters," has offered to accept my challenge to tell his pupils that they are as free to get up and go out of the school at any moment as their parents are to get up and go out of a theatre where my plays are being performed. Even among my own schoolmasters I can recollect a few whose classes interested me, and whom I should certainly have pestered for information and instruction if I could have got into any decent human relationship with them, and if they had not been compelled by their position to defend themselves as carefully against such advances as against furtive attempts to hurt them accidentally in the football field or smash their hats with a clod from behind a wall. But these rare cases actually do more harm than good; for they encourage us to pretend that all schoolmasters are like that. Of what use is it to us that there are always somewhere two or three teachers of children whose specific genius for their occupation triumphs over our tyrannous system and even finds in it its opportunity? For that matter, it is possible, if difficult, to find a solicitor, or even a judge, who has some notion of what law means, a doctor with a glimmering of science, an officer who understands duty and discipline, and a clergyman with an inkling of religion, though there are nothing like enough of them to go round. But even the few who, like Ibsen's Mrs Solness, have "a genius for nursing the souls of little children" are like angels forced to work in prisons instead of in heaven; and even at that they are mostly underpaid and despised. That friend of mine who went from the hedge schoolmaster to Harrow once saw a schoolmaster rush from an elementary school in pursuit of a boy and strike him. My friend, not considering that the unfortunate man was probably goaded beyond endurance, smote the schoolmaster and blackened his eye. The schoolmaster appealed to the law; and my friend found himself waiting nervously in the Hammersmith Police Court to answer for his breach of the peace. In his anxiety he asked a police officer what would happen to him. "What did you do?" said the officer. "I gave a man a black eye" said my friend. "Six pounds if he was a gentleman: two pounds if he wasnt," said the constable. "He was a schoolmaster" said my friend. "Two pounds" said the officer; and two pounds it was. The blood money was paid cheerfully; and I have ever since advised elementary schoolmasters to qualify themselves in the art of self-defence, as the British Constitution expresses our national estimate of them by allowing us to blacken three of their eyes for the same price as one of an ordinary professional man. How many Froebels and Pestalozzis and Miss Masons and Doctoress Montessoris would you be likely to get on these terms even if they occurred much more frequently in nature than they actually do?

No: I cannot be put off by the news that our system would be perfect if it were worked by angels. I do not admit it even at that, just as I do not admit that if the sky fell we should all catch larks. But I do not propose to bother about a supply of specific genius which does not exist, and which, if it did exist, could operate only by at once recognizing and establishing the rights of children.

WHAT WE DO NOT TEACH, AND WHY

To my mind, a glance at the subjects now taught in schools ought to convince any reasonable person that the object of the lessons is to keep children out of mischief, and not to qualify them for their part in life as responsible citizens of a free State. It is not possible to maintain freedom in any State, no matter how perfect its original constitution, unless its publicly active citizens know a good deal of constitutional history, law, and political science, with its basis of economics. If as much pains had been taken a century ago to make us all understand Ricardo's law of rent as to learn our catechisms, the face of the world would have been changed for the better. But for that very reason the greatest care is taken to keep such beneficially subversive knowledge from us, with the result that in public life we are either place-hunters, anarchists, or sheep shepherded by wolves.

But it will be observed that these are highly controversial subjects. Now no controversial subject can be taught dogmatically. He who knows only the official side of a controversy knows less than nothing of its nature. The abler a schoolmaster is, the more dangerous he is to his pupils unless they have the fullest opportunity of hearing another equally able person do his utmost to shake his authority and convict him of error.

At present such teaching is very unpopular. It does not exist in schools; but every adult who derives his knowledge of public affairs from the newspapers can take in, at the cost of an extra halfpenny, two papers of opposite politics. Yet the ordinary man so dislikes having his mind unsettled, as he calls it, that he angrily refuses to allow a paper which dissents from his views to be brought into his house. Even at his club he resents seeing it, and excludes it if it happens to run counter to the opinions of all the members. The result is that his opinions are not worth considering. A churchman who never reads The Freethinker very soon has no more real religion than the atheist who never reads The Church Times. The attitude is the same in both cases: they want to hear nothing good of their enemies; consequently they remain enemies and suffer from bad blood all their lives; whereas men who know their opponents and understand their case, quite commonly respect and like them, and always learn something from them.

Here, again, as at so many points, we come up against the abuse of schools to keep people in ignorance and error, so that they may be incapable of successful revolt against their industrial slavery. The most important simple fundamental economic truth to impress on a child in complicated civilizations like ours is the truth that whoever consumes goods or services without producing by personal effort the equivalent of what he or she consumes, inflicts on the community precisely the same injury that a thief produces, and would, in any honest State, be treated as a thief, however full his or her pockets might be of money made by other people. The nation that first teaches its children that truth, instead of flogging them if they discover it for themselves, may have to fight all the slaves of all the other nations to begin with; but it will beat them as easily as an unburdened man with his hands free and with all his energies in full play can beat an invalid who has to carry another invalid on his back.

This, however, is not an evil produced by the denial of children's rights, nor is it inherent in the nature of schools. I mention it only because it would be folly to call for a reform of our schools without taking account of the corrrupt resistance which awaits the reformer.

A word must also be said about the opposition to reform of the vested interest of the classical and coercive schoolmaster. He, poor wretch, has no other means of livelihood; and reform would leave him as a workman is now left when he is superseded by a machine. He had therefore better do what he can to get the workman compensated, so as to make the public familiar with the idea of compensation before his own turn comes.

TABOO IN SCHOOLS

The suppression of economic knowledge, disastrous as it is, is quite intelligible, its corrupt motive being as clear as the motive of a burglar for concealing his jemmy from a policeman. But the other great suppression in our schools, the suppression of the subject of sex, is a case of taboo. In mankind, the lower the type, and the less cultivated the mind, the less courage there is to face important subjects objectively. The ablest and most highly cultivated people continually discuss religion, politics, and sex: it is hardly an exaggeration to say that they discuss nothing else with fully-awakened interest. Commoner and less cultivated people, even when they form societies for discussion, make a rule that politics and religion are not to be mentioned, and take it for granted that no decent person would attempt to discuss sex. The three subjects are feared because they rouse the crude passions which call for furious gratification in murder and rapine at worst, and, at best, lead to quarrels and undesirable states of consciousness.

Even when this excuse of bad manners, ill temper, and brutishness (for that is what it comes to) compels us to accept it from those adults among whom political and theological discussion does as a matter of fact lead to the drawing of knives and pistols, and sex discussion leads to obscenity, it has no application to children except as an imperative reason for training them to respect other people's opinions, and to insist on respect for their own in these as in other important matters which are equally dangerous: for example, money. And in any case there are decisive reasons, superior, like the reasons for suspending conventional reticences between doctor and patient, to all considerations of mere decorum, for giving proper instruction in the facts of sex. Those who object to it (not counting coarse people who thoughtlessly seize every opportunity of affecting and parading a fictitious delicacy) are, in effect, advocating ignorance as a safeguard against precocity. If ignorance were practicable there would be something to be said for it up to the age at which ignorance is a danger instead of a safeguard. Even as it is, it seems undesirable that any special emphasis should be given to the subject, whether by way of delicacy and poetry or too impressive warning. But the plain fact is that in refusing to allow the child to be taught by qualified unrelated elders (the parents shrink from the lesson, even when they are otherwise qualified, because their own relation to the child makes the subject impossible between them) we are virtually arranging to have our children taught by other children in guilty secrets and unclean jests. And that settles the question for all sensible people.

The dogmatic objection, the sheer instinctive taboo which rules the subject out altogether as indecent, has no age limit. It means that at no matter what age a woman consents to a proposal of marriage, she should do so in ignorance of the relation she is undertaking. When this actually happens (and apparently it does happen oftener than would seem possible) a horrible fraud is being practised on both the man and the woman. He is led to believe that she knows what she is promising, and that he is in no danger of finding himself bound to a woman to whom he is eugenically antipathetic. She contemplates nothing but such affectionate relations as may exist between her and her nearest kinsmen, and has no knowledge of the condition which, if not foreseen, must come as an amazing revelation and a dangerous shock, ending possibly in the discovery that the marriage has been an irreparable mistake. Nothing can justify such a risk. There may be people incapable of understanding that the right to know all there is to know about oneself is a natural human right that sweeps away all the pretences of others to tamper with one's consciousness in order to produce what they choose to consider a good character. But they must here bow to the plain mischievousness of entrapping people into contracts on which the happiness of their whole lives depends without letting them know what they are undertaking.

ALLEGED NOVELTIES IN MODERN SCHOOLS

There is just one more nuisance to be disposed of before I come to the positive side of my case. I mean the person who tells me that my schooldays belong to a bygone order of educational ideas and institutions, and that schools are not now a bit like my old school. I reply, with Sir Walter Raleigh, by calling on my soul to give this statement the lie. Some years ago I lectured in Oxford on the subject of Education. A friend to whom I mentioned my intention said, "You know nothing of modern education: schools are not now what they were when you were a boy." I immediately procured the time sheets of half a dozen modern schools, and found, as I expected, that they might all have been my old school: there was no real difference. I may mention, too, that I have visited modern schools, and observed that there is a tendency to hang printed pictures in an untidy and soulless manner on the walls, and occasionally to display on the mantelshelf a deplorable glass case containing certain objects which might possibly, if placed in the hands of the pupils, give them some practical experience of the weight of a pound and the length of an inch. And sometimes a scoundrel who has rifled a bird's nest or killed a harmless snake encourages the children to go and do likewise by putting his victims into an imitation nest and bottling and exhibiting them as aids to "Nature study." A suggestion that Nature is worth study would certainly have staggered my schoolmasters; so perhaps I may admit a gleam of progress here. But as any child who attempted to handle these these dusty objects would probably be caned, I do not attach any importance to such modernities in school furniture. The school remains what it was in my boyhood, because its real object remains what it was. And that object, I repeat, is to keep the children out of mischief: mischief meaning for the most part worrying the grownups.

WHAT IS TO BE DONE?

The practical question, then, is what to do with the children. Tolerate them at home we will not. Let them run loose in the streets we dare not until our streets become safe places for children, which, to our utter shame, they are not at present, though they can hardly be worse than some homes and some schools.

The grotesque difficulty of making even a beginning was brought home to me by the lady of the manor in the little village in Hertfordshire where I write these lines. She asked me very properly what I was going to do for the village school. I did not know what to reply. As the school kept the children quiet during my working hours, I did not for the sake of my own personal convenience want to blow it up with dynamite as I should like to blow up most schools. So I asked for guidance. "You ought to give a prize" said the lady. I asked if there was a prize for good conduct. As I expected, there was: one for the best-behaved boy and another for the best-behaved girl. On reflection I offered a handsome prize for the worst-behaved boy and girl on condition that a record should be kept of their subsequent careers and compared with the records of the best-behaved, in order to ascertain whether the school criterion of good conduct was valid out of school. My offer was refused because it would not have had the effect of encouraging the children to give as little trouble as possible, which is of course the real object of all conduct prizes in schools.

I must not pretend, then, that I have a system ready to replace all the other systems. Obstructing the way of the proper organization of childhood, as of everything else, lies our ridiculous misdistribution of the national income, with its accompanying class distinctions and imposition of snobbery on children as a necessary part of their social training. The result of our economic folly is that we are a nation of undesirable acquaintances; and the first object of all our institutions for children is segregation. If, for example, our children were set free to roam and play about as they pleased, they would have to be policed; and the first duty of the police in a State like ours would be to see that every child wore a badge indicating its class in society, and that every child seen speaking to another child with a lower-class badge, or any child wearing a higher badge than that allotted to it by, say, the College of Heralds, should immediately be skinned alive with a birch rod. It might even be insisted that girls with high-class badges should be attended by footmen, grooms, or even military escorts. In short, there is hardly any limit to the follies with which our Commercialism would infect any system that it would tolerate at all. But something like a change of heart is still possible; and since all the evils of snobbery and segregation are rampant in our schools at present we may as well make the best as the worst of them.

CHILDREN'S RIGHTS AND DUTIES

Now let us ask what are a child's rights, and what are the rights of society over the child. Its rights, being clearly those of any other human being, are summed up in the right to live: that is, to have all the conclusive arguments that prove that it would be better dead, that it is a child of wrath, that the population is already excessive, that the pains of life are greater than its pleasures, that its sacrifice in a hospital or laboratory experiment might save millions of lives, etc. etc. etc., put out of the question, and its existence accepted as necessary and sacred, all theories to the contrary notwithstanding, whether by Calvin or Schopenhauer or Pasteur or the nearest person with a taste for infanticide. And this right to live includes, and in fact is, the right to be what the child likes and can, to do what it likes and can, to make what it likes and can, to think what it likes and can, to smash what it dislikes and can, and generally to behave in an altogether unaccountable manner within the limits imposed by the similar rights of its neighbors. And the rights of society over it clearly extend to requiring it to qualify itself to live in society without wasting other people's time: that is, it must know the rules of the road, be able to read placards and proclamations, fill voting papers, compose and send letters and telegrams, purchase food and clothing and railway tickets for itself, count money and give and take change, and, generally, know how many beans make five. It must know some law, were it only a simple set of commandments, some political economy, agriculture enough to shut the gates of fields with cattle in them and not to trample on growing crops, sanitation enough not to defile its haunts, and religion enough to have some idea of why it is allowed its rights and why it must respect the rights of others. And the rest of its education must consist of anything else it can pick up; for beyond this society cannot go with any certainty, and indeed can only go this far rather apologetically and provisionally, as doing the best it can on very uncertain ground.

SHOULD CHILDREN EARN THEIR LIVING?

Now comes the question how far children should be asked to contribute to the support of the community. In approaching it we must put aside the considerations that now induce all humane and thoughtful political students to agitate for the uncompromising abolition of child labor under our capitalist system. It is not the least of the curses of that system that it will bequeath to future generations a mass of legislation to prevent capitalists from "using up nine generations of men in one generation," as they began by doing until they were restrained by law at the suggestion of Robert Owen, the founder of English Socialism. Most of this legislation will become an insufferable restraint upon freedom and variety of action when Capitalism goes the way of Druidic human sacrifice (a much less slaughterous institution). There is every reason why a child should not be allowed to work for commercial profit or for the support of its parents at the expense of its own future; but there is no reason whatever why a child should not do some work for its own sake and that of the community if it can be shewn that both it and the community will be the better for it.

Also it is important to put the happiness of the children rather carefully in its place, which is really not a front place. The unsympathetic, selfish, hard people who regard happiness as a very exceptional indulgence to which children are by no means entitled, though they may be allowed a very little of it on their birthdays or at Christmas, are sometimes better parents in effect than those who imagine that children are as capable of happiness as adults. Adults habitually exaggerate their own capacity in that direction grossly; yet most adults can stand an allowance of happiness that would be quite thrown away on children. The secret of being miserable is to have leisure to bother about whether you are happy or not. The cure for it is occupation, because occupation means pre-occupation; and the pre-occupied person is neither happy nor unhappy, but simply alive and active, which is pleasanter than any happiness until you are tired of it. That is why it is necessary to happiness that one should be tired. Music after dinner is pleasant: music before breakfast is so unpleasant as to be clearly unnatural. To people who are not overworked holidays are a nuisance. To people who are, and who can afford them, they are a troublesome necessity. A perpetual holiday is a good working definition of hell.

It will be said here that, on the contrary, heaven is always conceived as a perpetual holiday, and that whoever is not born to an independent income is striving for one or longing for one because it gives holidays for life. To which I reply, first, that heaven, as conventionally conceived, is a place so inane, so dull, so useless, so miserable, that nobody has ever ventured to describe a whole day in heaven, though plenty of people have described a day at the seaside; and that the genuine popular verdict on it is expressed in the proverb "Heaven for holiness and Hell for company." Second, I point out that the wretched people who have independent incomes and no useful occupation, do the most amazingly disagreeable and dangerous things to make themselves tired and hungry in the evening. When they are not involved in what they call sport, they are doing aimlessly what other people have to be paid to do: driving horses and motor cars; trying on dresses and walking up and down to shew them off; and acting at footmen and housemaids to royal personages. The sole and obvious cause of the notion that idleness is delightful and that heaven is a place where there is nothing to be done, is our school system and our industrial system. The school is a prison in which work is a punishment and a curse. In avowed prisons, hard labor, the only alleviation of a prisoner's lot, is treated as an aggravation of his punishment; and everything possible is done to intensify the prisoner's inculcated and unnatural notion that work is an evil. In industry we are overworked and underfed prisoners. Under such absurd circumstances our judgment of things becomes as perverted as our habits. If we were habitually underworked and overfed, our notion of heaven would be a place where everybody worked strenuously for twenty-four hours a day and never got anything to eat.

Once realize that a perpetual holiday is beyond human endurance, and that "Satan finds some mischief still for idle hands to do" and it will be seen that we have no right to impose a perpetual holiday on children. If we did, they would soon outdo the Labor Party in the claim for a Right to Work Bill.

In any case no child should be brought up to suppose that its food and clothes come down from heaven or are miraculously conjured from empty space by papa. Loathsome as we have made the idea of duty (like the idea of work) we must habituate children to a sense of repayable obligation to the community for what they consume and enjoy, and inculcate the repayment as a point of honor. If we did that today—and nothing but flat dishonesty prevents us from doing it—we should have no idle rich and indeed probably no rich, since there is no distinction in being rich if you have to pay scot and lot in personal effort like the working folk. Therefore, if for only half an hour a day, a child should do something serviceable to the community.

Productive work for children has the advantage that its discipline is the discipline of impersonal necessity, not that of wanton personal coercion. The eagerness of children in our industrial districts to escape from school to the factory is not caused by lighter tasks or shorter hours in the factory, nor altogether by the temptation of wages, nor even by the desire for novelty, but by the dignity of adult work, the exchange of the humiliating liability to personal assault from the lawless schoolmaster, from which the grown-ups are free, for the stern but entirely dignified pressure of necessity to which all flesh is subject.

UNIVERSITY SCHOOLBOYISHNESS

Older children might do a good deal before beginning their collegiate education. What is the matter with our universities is that the students are school children, whereas it is of the very essence of university education that they should be adults. The function of a university is not to teach things that can now be taught as well or better by University Extension lectures or by private tutors or modern correspondence classes with gramophones. We go to them to be socialized: to acquire the hall mark of communal training; to become citizens of the world instead of inmates of the enlarged rabbit hutches we call homes; to learn manners and become unchallengeable ladies and gentlemen. The social pressure which effects these changes should be that of persons who have faced the full responsibilities of adults as working members of the general community, not that of a rowdy rabble of half emancipated school children and unemancipable pedants. It is true that in a reasonable state of society this outside experience would do for us very completely what the university does now so corruptly that we tolerate its bad manners only because they are better than no manners at all. But the university will always exist in some form as a community of persons desirous of pushing their culture to the highest pitch they are capable of, not as solitary students reading in seclusion, but as members of a body of individuals all pursuing culture, talking culture, thinking culture, above all, criticizing culture. If such persons are to read and talk and criticize to any purpose, they must know the world outside the university at least as well as the shopkeeper in the High Street does. And this is just what they do not know at present. You may say of them, paraphrasing Mr Kipling, "What do they know of Plato that only Plato know?" If our universities would exclude everybody who had not earned a living by his or her own exertions for at least a couple of years, their effect would be vastly improved.

THE NEW LAZINESS

The child of the future, then, if there is to be any future but one of decay, will work more or less for its living from an early age; and in doing so it will not shock anyone, provided there be no longer any reason to associate the conception of children working for their living with infants toiling in a factory for ten hours a day or boys drudging from nine to six under gas lamps in underground city offices. Lads and lasses in their teens will probably be able to produce as much as the most expensive person now costs in his own person (it is retinue that eats up the big income) without working too hard or too long for quite as much happiness as they can enjoy. The question to be balanced then will be, not how soon people

should be put to work, but how soon they should be re-
leased from any obligation of the kind. A life's work is
like a day's work: it can begin early and leave off early
or begin late and leave off late, or, as with us, begin too
early and never leave off at all, obviously the worst of
all possible plans. In any event we must finally reckon
work, not as the curse our schools and prisons and
capitalist profit factories make it seem today, but as a
prime necessity of a tolerable existence. And if we cannot
devise fresh wants as fast as we shorten the process of
supplying the old ones, there will come a scarcity of work
simultaneously with an excess of leisure. Work may have
to be shared out among people who want more of it. Our
spurious substitute, exercise, will not serve. A new sort of
laziness will become the bugbear of society: the laziness
that refuses to face the mental toil and adventure of
making work by inventing new ideas or extending the
domain of knowledge, and insists on a ready-made routine. It may come to forcing people to retire before they
are willing to make way for younger ones: that is, to
driving all persons of a certain age out of industry, leaving
them to find something experimental to occupy them on
pain of perpetual holiday. Men will then try to spend
twenty thousand a year for the sake of having to earn it.
Instead of being what we are now, the cheapest and
nastiest of the animals, we shall be the costliest, most
fastidious, and best bred. In short, there is no end to the
astonishing things that may happen when the curse of
Adam becomes first a blessing and then an incurable
habit. And in view of that day we must not grudge children their share of it.

THE INFINITE SCHOOL TASK

The question of children's work, however, is only a question of what the child ought to do for the community.
How highly it should qualify itself is another matter. But
most of the difficulty of inducing children to learn would

disappear if our demands became not only definite but finite. When learning is only an excuse for imprisonment, it is an instrument of torture which becomes more painful the more progress is made. Thus when you have forced a child to learn the Church Catechism, a document profound beyond the comprehension of most adults, you are sometimes at a standstill for something else to teach; and you therefore keep the wretched child repeating its catechism again and again until you hit on the plan of making it learn instalments of Bible verses, preferably from the book of Numbers. But as it is less trouble to set a lesson that you know yourself, there is a tendency to keep repeating the already learnt lesson rather than break new ground. At school I began with a fairly complete knowledge of Latin grammar in the childish sense of being able to repeat all the paradigms; and I was kept at this, or rather kept in a class where the master never asked me to do it because he knew I could, and therefore devoted himself to trapping the boys who could not, until I finally forgot most of it. But when progress took place, what did it mean? First it meant Caesar, with the foreknowledge that to master Caesar meant only being set at Virgil, with the culminating horror of Greek and Homer in reserve at the end of that. I preferred Caesar, because his statement that Gaul is divided into three parts, though neither interesting nor true, was the only Latin sentence I could translate at sight: therefore the longer we stuck at Caesar the better I was pleased. Just so do less classically educated children see nothing in the mastery of addition but the beginning of subtraction, and so on through multiplication and division and fractions, with the black cloud of algebra on the horizon. And if a boy rushes through all that, there is always the calculus to fall back on, unless indeed you insist on his learning music, and proceed to hit him if he cannot tell you the year Beethoven was born.

A child has a right to finality as regards its compulsory lessons. Also as regards physical training. At present it is assumed that the schoolmaster has a right to force every child into an attempt to become Porson and Bentley, Leibnitz and Newton, all rolled into one. This is the tradition of the oldest grammar schools. In our times an even more horrible and cynical claim has been made for the right to drive boys through compulsory games in the playing fields until they are too much exhausted physically to do anything but drop off to sleep. This is supposed to protect them from vice; but as it also protects them from poetry, literature, music, meditation and prayer, it may be dismissed with the obvious remark that if boarding schools are places whose keepers are driven to such monstrous measures lest more abominable things should happen, then the sooner boarding schools are violently abolished the better. It is true that society may make physical claims on the child as well as mental ones: the child must learn to walk, to use a knife and fork, to swim, to ride a bicycle, to acquire sufficient power of self-defence to make an attack on it an arduous and uncertain enterprise, perhaps to fly. What as a matter of common sense it clearly has not a right to do is to make this an excuse for keeping the child slaving for ten hours at physical exercises on the ground that it is not yet as dexterous as Cinquevalli and as strong as Sandow.

THE REWARDS AND RISKS OF KNOWLEDGE

In a word, we cannot completely educate a child; for its education can end only with its life and will not even then be complete. Compulsory completion of education is the last folly of a rotten and desperate civilization. All we can fairly do is to prescribe definite acquirements and accomplishments as qualifications for citizenship in general, with further specific qualifications for professional employments; and to secure them, not by the ridiculous method of inflicting artificial injuries on the persons who have not yet mastered them, but by the natural co-operation of self-respect from within with social respect from without.

Most acquirements carry their own privileges with them. Thus a baby has to be pretty closely guarded and imprisoned because it cannot take care of itself. It has even to be carried about (the most complete conceivable infringement of its liberty) until it can walk. But nobody goes on carrying children after they can walk lest they should walk into mischief, though Arab boys make their sisters carry them, as our own spoiled children sometimes make their nurses, out of mere laziness, because sisters in the East and nurses in the West are kept in servitude. But in a society of equals (the only reasonable and permanently possible sort of society) children are in much greater danger of acquiring bandy legs through being left to walk before they are strong enough than of being carried when they are well able to walk. Anyhow, freedom of movement in a nursery is the reward of learning to walk; and in precisely the same way freedom of movement in a city is the reward of learning how to read public notices, and to count and use money. The consequences are of course much larger than the mere ability to read the name of a street or the number of a railway platform and the destination of a train. When you enable a child to read these, you also enable it to read this preface, to the utter destruction, you may quite possibly think, of its morals (its docility). You also expose it to the danger of being run over by taxicabs and trains. The moral and physical risks of education are enormous: every new power a child acquires, from speaking, walking, and co-ordinating its vision, to conquering continents and founding religions, opens up immense new possibilities of mischief. Teach a child to write and you teach it how to forge: teach it to speak and you teach it how to lie: teach it to walk and you teach it how to kick its mother to death.

The great problem of slavery for those whose aim is to maintain it is the problem of reconciling the efficiency of the slave with the helplessness that keeps him in servitude; and this problem is fortunately not completely soluble;

for it is not in fact found possible for a duke to treat his solicitor or his doctor as he treats his laborers, though they are all equally his slaves: the laborer being in fact less dependent on his favor than the professional man. Hence it is that men come to resent, of all things, protection, because it so often means restriction of their liberty lest they should make a bad use of it. If there are dangerous precipices about, it is much easier and cheaper to forbid people to walk near the edge than to put up an effective fence: that is why both legislators and parents and the paid deputies of parents are always inhibiting and prohibiting and punishing and scolding and laming and cramping and delaying progress and growth instead of making the dangerous places as safe as possible and then boldly taking and allowing others to take the irreducible minimum of risk.

ENGLISH PHYSICAL HARDIHOOD AND SPIRITUAL COWARDICE

It is easier to convert most people to the need for allowing their children to run physical risks than moral ones. I can remember a relative of mine who, when I was a small child, unused to horses and very much afraid of them, insisted on putting me on a rather rumbustious pony with little spurs on my heels (knowing that in my agitation I would use them unconsciously), and being enormously amused at my terrors. Yet when that same lady discovered that I had found a copy of The Arabian Nights and was devouring it with avidity, she was horrified, and hid it away from me lest it should break my soul as the pony might have broken my neck. This way of producing hardy bodies and timid souls is so common in country-houses that you may spend hours in them listening to stories of broken collar bones, broken backs, and broken necks without coming upon a single spiritual adventure or daring thought.

But whether the risks to which liberty exposes us are

moral or physical, our right to liberty involves the right to run them. A man who is not free to risk his neck as an aviator or his soul as a heretic is not free at all; and the right to liberty begins, not at the age of 21 years but of 21 seconds.

THE RISKS OF IGNORANCE AND WEAKNESS

The difficulty with children is that they need protection from risks they are too young to understand, and attacks they can neither avoid nor resist. You may on academic grounds allow a child to snatch glowing coals from the fire once. You will not do it twice. The risks of liberty we must let everyone take; but the risks of ignorance and self-helplessness are another matter. Not only children but adults need protection from them. At present adults are often exposed to risks outside their knowledge or beyond their comprehension or powers of resistance or foresight: for example, we have to look on every day at marriages or financial speculations that may involve far worse consequences than burnt fingers. And just as it is part of the business of adults to protect children, to feed them, clothe them, shelter them, and shift for them in all sorts of ways until they are able to shift for themselves, it is coming more and more to be seen that this is true not only of the relation between adults and children, but between adults and adults. We shall not always look on indifferently at foolish marriages and financial speculations, nor allow dead men to control live communities by ridiculous wills and living heirs to squander and ruin great estates, nor tolerate a hundred other absurd liberties that we allow today because we are too lazy to find out the proper way to interfere. But the interference must be regulated by some theory of the individual's rights. Though the right to live is absolute, it is not unconditional. If a man is unbearably mischievous, he must be killed. This is a mere matter of necessity, like the killing of a man-eating tiger in a nursery, a venomous snake in the garden, or a fox in the poultry yard. No society could be constructed on the assumption that such extermination is a violation of the creature's right to live, and therefore must not be allowed. And then at once arises the danger into which morality has led us: the danger of persecution. One Christian spreading his doctrines may seem more mischievous than a dozen thieves: throw him therefore to the lions. A lying or disobedient child may corrupt a whole generation and make human Society impossible: therefore thrash the vice out of him. And so on until our whole system of abortion, intimidation, tyranny, cruelty, and the rest is in full swing again.

THE COMMON SENSE OF TOLERATION

The real safeguard against this is the dogma of Toleration. I need not here repeat the compact treatise on it which I prepared for the Joint Committee on the Censorship of Stage Plays, and prefixed to The Shewing Up of Blanco Posnet. It must suffice now to say that the present must not attempt to schoolmaster the future by pretending to know good from evil in tendency, or protect citizens against shocks to their opinions and convictions, moral, political or religious: in other words it must not persecute doctrines of any kind, or what is called bad taste, and must insist on all persons facing such shocks as they face frosty weather or any of the other disagreeable, dangerous, or bracing incidents of freedom. The expediency of Toleration has been forced on us by the fact that progressive enlightenment depends on a fair hearing for doctrines which at first appear seditious, blasphemous, and immoral, and which deeply shock people who never think originally, thought being with them merely a habit and an echo. The deeper ground for Toleration is the nature of creation, which, as we now know, proceeds by evolution. Evolution finds its way by experiment; and this finding of the way varies according to the stage of development reached, from the blindest groping along the line of least resistance to conscious intellectual speculation, with its routine of hypothesis and verification, induction and deduction; or even into so rapid and intuitive an integration of all these processes in a single brain that we get the inspired guess of the man of genius and the fanatical resolution of the teacher of new truths who is first slain as a blasphemous apostate and then worshipped as a prophet.

Here the law for the child is the same as for the adult. The high priest must not rend his garments and cry "Crucify him" when he is shocked, nor the atheist clamor for the suppression of Law's Serious Call because it has for two centuries destroyed the natural happiness of innumerable children by persuading pious parents that it is a religious duty to make children miserable. It, and the Sermon on the Mount, and Machiavelli's Prince, and La Rochefoucauld's maxims, and Hymns Ancient and Modern, and De Glanville's apologue, and Dr. Watts's rhymes, and Neitzsche's Gay Science, and Ingersoll's Mistakes of Moses, and the speeches and pamphlets of the people who want us to make war on Germany, and the Noodle's Orations and articles of our politicians and journalists, must all be tolerated not only because any of them may for all we know be on the right track but because it is in the conflict of opinion that we win knowledge and wisdom. However terrible the wounds suffered in that conflict, they are better than the barren peace of death that follows when all the combatants are slaughtered or bound hand and foot.

The difficulty at present is that though this necessity for Toleration is a law of political science as well established as the law of gravitation, our rulers are never taught political science: on the contrary, they are taught in school that the master tolerates nothing that is disagreeable to him; that ruling is simply being master; and that the master's method is the method of violent punishment. And our citizens, all school taught, are walking in the same darkness. As I write these lines the Home

Secretary is explaining that he must not release a man who has been imprisoned for blasphemy, as his remarks were painful to the feelings of his pious fellow-townsmen. Now it happens that this very Home Secretary has driven many thousands of his fellow-citizens almost beside themselves by the crudity of his notions of government, and his simple inability to understand why he should not use and make laws to torment and subdue people who do not happen to agree with him. In a word, he is not a politician, but a grown-up schoolboy who has at last got a cane in his hand. And as all the rest of us are in the same condition (except as to command of the cane) the only objection made to his proceedings takes the shape of clamorous demands that *he* should be caned instead of being allowed to cane other people.

THE SIN OF ATHANASIUS

It seems hopeless. Anarchists are tempted to preach a violent and implacable resistance to all law as the only remedy; and the result of that speedily is that people welcome any tyranny that will rescue them from chaos. But there is really no need to choose between anarchy and tyranny. A quite reasonable state of things is practicable if we proceed on human assumptions and not on academic ones. If adults will frankly give up their claim to know better than children what the purposes of the Life Force are, and treat the child as an experiment like themselves, and possibly a more successful one, and at the same time relinquish their monstrous parental claims to personal private property in children, the rest may be left to common sense. It is our attitude, our religion, that is wrong. A good beginning might be made by enacting that any person dictating a piece of conduct to a child or to anyone else as the will of God, or as absolutely right, should be dealt with as a blasphemer: as, indeed, guilty of the unpardonable sin against the Holy Ghost. If the penalty were death, it would rid us at once of that scourge of humanity, the amateur Pope. As an Irish Protestant, I raise the cry of No Popery with hereditary zest. We are overrun with Popes. From curates and governesses, who may claim a sort of professional standing, to parents and uncles and nurserymaids and school teachers and wiseacres generally, there are scores of thousands of human insects groping through our darkness by the feeble phosphorescence of their own tails, yet ready at a moment's notice to reveal the will of God on every possible subject; to explain how and why the universe was made (in my youth they added the exact date) and the circumstances under which it will cease to exist; to lay down precise rules of right and wrong conduct; to discriminate infallibly between virtuous and vicious character; and this with such certainty that they are prepared to visit all the rigors of the law, and all the ruinous penalties of social ostracism on those, however harmless their actions may be, who venture to laugh at their monstrous conceit or to pay their assumptions the extravagant compliment of criticizing them. As to children, who shall say what canings and birchings and terrifyings and threats of hell fire and impositions and humiliations and petty imprisonings and sendings to bed and standing in corners and the like they have suffered because their parents and guardians and teachers knew everything so much better than Socrates or Solon?

It is this ignorant uppishness that does the mischief. A stranger on the planet might expect that its grotesque absurdity would provoke enough ridicule to cure it; but unfortunately quite the contrary happens. Just as our ill health delivers us into the hands of medical quacks and creates a passionate demand for impudent pretences that doctors can cure the diseases they themselves die of daily, so our ignorance and helplessness set us clamoring for spiritual and moral quacks who pretend that they can save our souls from their own damnation. If a doctor were to say to his patients, "I am familiar with your symptoms, because I have seen other people in your condition; and

I will bring the very little knowledge we have to your treatment; but except in that very shallow sense I dont know what is the matter with you; and I cant undertake to cure you" he would be a lost man professionally; and if a clergyman, on being called on to award a prize for good conduct in the village school, were to say, "I am afraid I cannot say who is the best-behaved child, because I really do not know what good conduct is; but I will gladly take the teacher's word as to which child has caused least inconvenience" he would probably be unfrocked, if not excommunicated. And yet no honest and intellectually capable doctor or parson can say more. Clearly it would not be wise of the doctor to say it, because optimistic lies have such immense therapeutic value that a doctor who cannot tell them convincingly has mistaken his profession. And a clergyman who is not prepared to lay down the law dogmatically will not be of much use in a village school, though it behoves him all the more to be very careful what law he lays down. But unless both the clergyman and the doctor are in the attitude expressed by these speeches they are not fit for their work. The man who believes that he has more than a provisional hypothesis to go upon is a born fool. He may have to act vigorously on it. The world has no use for the Agnostic who wont believe anything because anything might be false, and wont deny anything because anything might be true. But there is a wide difference between saying, "I believe this; and I am going to act on it," or, "I dont believe it; and I wont act on it," and saying, "It is true; and it is my duty and yours to act on it," or, "It is false; and it is my duty and yours to refuse to act on it." The difference is as great as that between the Apostles' Creed and the Athanasian Creed. When you repeat the Apostles' Creed you affirm that you believe certain things. There you are clearly within your rights. When you repeat the Athanasian Creed, you affirm that certain things are so, and that anybody who doubts that they are so cannot be saved. And this is simply a piece of impudence on your part, as you know nothing about it except that as good men as you have never heard of your creed. The apostolic attitude is a desire to convert others to our beliefs for the sake of sympathy and light: the Athanasian attitude is a desire to murder people who dont agree with us. I am sufficient of an Athanasian to advocate a law for the speedy execution of all Athanasians, because they violate the fundamental proposition of my creed, which is, I repeat, that all living creatures are experiments. The precise formula for the Superman, *ci-devant* The Just Man Made Perfect, has not yet been discovered. Until it is, every birth is an experiment in the Great Research which is being conducted by the Life Force to discover that formula.

THE EXPERIMENT EXPERIMENTING

And now all the modern schoolmaster abortionists will rise up beaming, and say, "We quite agree. We regard every child in our school as a subject for experiment. We are always experimenting with them. We challenge the experimental test for our system. We are continually guided by our experience in our great work of moulding the character of our future citizens, etc. etc. etc." I am sorry to seem irreconcilable; but it is the Life Force that has to make the experiment and not the schoolmaster; and the Life Force for the child's purpose is in the child and not in the schoolmaster. The schoolmaster is another experiment; and a laboratory in which all the experiments began experimenting on one another would not produce intelligible results. I admit, however, that if my schoolmasters had treated me as an experiment of the Life Force: that is, if they had set me free to do as I liked subject only to my political rights and theirs, they could not have watched the experiment very long, because the first result would have been a rapid movement on my part in the direction of the door, and my disappearance therethrough.

It may be worth inquiring where I should have gone to. I should say that practically every time I should have gone to a much more educational place. I should have gone into the country, or into the sea, or into the National Gallery, or to hear a band if there was one, or to any library where there were no schoolbooks. I should have read very dry and difficult books: for example, though nothing would have induced me to read the budget of stupid party lies that served as a text-book of history in school, I remember reading Robertson's Charles V. and his history of Scotland from end to end most laboriously. Once, stung by the airs of a schoolfellow who alleged that he had read Locke On The Human Understanding, I attempted to read the Bible straight through, and actually got to the Pauline Epistles before I broke down in disgust at what seemed to me their inveterate crookedness of mind. If there had been a school where children were really free, I should have had to be driven out of it for the sake of my health by the teachers; for the children to whom a literary education can be of any use are insatiable: they will read and study far more than is good for them. In fact the real difficulty is to prevent them from wasting their time by reading for the sake of reading and studying for the sake of studying, instead of taking some trouble to find out what they really like and are capable of doing some good at. Some silly person will probably interrupt me here with the remark that many children have no appetite for a literary education at all, and would never open a book if they were not forced to. I have known many such persons who have been forced to the point of obtaining university degrees. And for all the effect their literary exercises has left on them they might just as well have been put on the treadmill. In fact they are actually less literate than the treadmill would have left them; for they might now by chance pick up and dip into a volume of Shakespear or a translation of Homer if they had not been driven to loathe every famous name in literature. I should probably know as much Latin as

French, if Latin had not been made the excuse for my school imprisonment and degradation.

WHY WE LOATHE LEARNING AND LOVE SPORT

If we are to discuss the importance of art, learning, and intellectual culture, the first thing we have to recognize is that we have very little of them at present; and that this little has not been produced by compulsory education; nay, that the scarcity is unnatural and has been produced by the violent exclusion of art and artists from schools. On the other hand we have quite a considerable degree of bodily culture: indeed there is a continual outcry against the sacrifice of mental accomplishments to athletics. In other words a sacrifice of the professed object of compulsory education to the real object of voluntary education. It is assumed that this means that people prefer bodily to mental culture; but may it not mean that they prefer liberty and satisfaction to coercion and privation. Why is it that people who have been taught Shakespear as a school subject loathe his plays and cannot by any means be persuaded ever to open his works after they escape from school, whereas there is still, 300 years after his death, a wide and steady sale for his works to people who regard his plays as plays, not as task work? If Shakespear, or for that matter, Newton and Leibnitz, are allowed to find their readers and students they will find them. If their works are annotated and paraphrased by dullards, and the annotations and paraphrases forced on all young people by imprisonment and flogging and scolding, there will not be a single man of letters or higher mathematician the more in the country: on the contrary there will be less, as so many potential lovers of literature and mathematics will have been incurably prejudiced against them. Everyone who is conversant with the class in which child imprisonment and compulsory schooling is carried out to the final extremity of the university degree knows that its scholastic culture is a sham; that it knows little about literature or art and a great deal about point-to-point races; and that the village cobbler, who has never read a page of Plato, and is admittedly a dangerously ignorant man politically, is nevertheless a Socrates compared to the classically educated gentlemen who discuss politics in country-houses at election time (and at no other time) after their day's earnest and skilful shooting. Think of the years and years of weary torment the women of the piano-possessing class have been forced to spend over the keyboard, fingering scales. How many of them could be bribed to attend a pianoforte recital by a great player, though they will rise from sick beds rather than miss Ascot or Goodwood?

Another familiar fact that teaches the same lesson is that many women who have voluntarily attained a high degree of culture cannot add up their own housekeeping books, though their education in simple arithmetic was compulsory, whereas their higher education has been wholly voluntary. Everywhere we find the same result. The imprisonment, the beating, the taming and laming, the breaking of young spirits, the arrest of development, the atrophy of all inhibitive power except the power of fear, are real: the education is sham. Those who have been taught most know least.

ANTICHRIST

Among the worst effects of the unnatural segregation of children in schools and the equally unnatural constant association of them with adults in the family is the utter defeat of the vital element in Christianity. Christ stands in the world for that intuition of the highest humanity that we, being members one of another, must not complain, must not scold, must not strike, nor revile nor persecute nor revenge nor punish. Now family life and school life are, as far as the moral training of children is concerned, nothing but the deliberate inculcation of a routine of complaint, scolding, punishment, persecution, and revenge as the natural and only possible way of dealing with evil or inconvenience. "Aint nobody to be whopped for this here?" exclaimed Sam Weller when he saw his employer's name written up on a stage coach, and conceived the phenomenon as an insult which reflected on himself. This exclamation of Sam Weller is at once the negation of Christianity and the beginning and the end of current morality; and so it will remain as long as the family and the school persist as we know them: that is, as long as the rights of children are so utterly denied that nobody will even take the trouble to ascertain what they are, and coming of age is like the turning of a convict into the streets after twenty-one years penal servitude. Indeed it is worse; for the convict, having learnt before his conviction how to live at large, may remember how to set about it, however lamed his power of initiative may have become through disuse; but the child knows no other way of life than the slave's way. Born free, as Rousseau says, he has been laid hands on by slaves from the moment of his birth and brought up as a slave. How is he, when he is at last set free, to be anything else than the slave he actually is, clamoring for war, for the lash, for police, prisons, and scaffolds in a wild panic of delusion that without these things he is lost. The grown-up Englishman is to the end of his days a badly brought-up child, beyond belief quarrelsome, petulant, selfish, destructive, and cowardly: afraid that the Germans will come and enslave him; that the burglar will come and rob him; that the bicycle or motor car will run over him; that the smallpox will attack him; and that the devil will run away with him and empty him out like a sack of coals on a blazing fire unless his nurse or his parents or his schoolmaster or his bishop or his judge or his army or his navy will do something to frighten these bad things away. And this Englishman, without the moral courage of a louse, will risk his neck for fun fifty times every winter in the hunting field, and at Badajos sieges and the like will ram his head into a hole bristling with sword blades rather than be beaten in the one department in which he has been brought up to consult his own honor. As a Sportsman (and war is fundamentally the sport of hunting and fighting the most dangerous of the beasts of prey) he feels free. He will tell you himself that the true sportsman is never a snob, a coward, a duffer, a cheat, a thief, or a liar. Curious, is it not, that he has not the same confidence in other sorts of man?

And even sport is losing its freedom. Soon everybody will be schooled, mentally and physically, from the cradle to the end of the term of adult compulsory military service, and finally of compulsory civil service lasting until the age of superannuation. Always more schooling, more compulsion. We are to be cured by an excess of the dose that has poisoned us. Satan is to cast out Satan.

UNDER THE WHIP

Clearly this will not do. We must reconcile education with liberty. We must find out some means of making men workers and, if need be, warriors, without making them slaves. We must cultivate the noble virtues that have their root in pride. Now no schoolmaster will teach these any more than a prison governor will teach his prisoners how to mutiny and escape. Self-preservation forces him to break the spirit that revolts against him, and to inculcate submission, even to obscene assault, as a duty. A bishop once had the hardihood to say that he would rather see England free than England sober. Nobody has yet dared to say that he would rather see an England of ignoramuses than an England of cowards and slaves. And if anyone did, it would be necessary to point out that the antithesis is not a practical one, as we have at present an England of ignoramuses who are also cowards and slaves, and patriotically proud of it at that, because in school they are taught to submit, with what they ridiculously call Oriental fatalism (as if any Oriental has ever submitted more helplessly and sheepishly to robbery and oppression than we Occidentals do), to be driven day after day into compounds and set to the tasks they loathe by the men they hate and fear, as if this were the inevitable destiny of mankind. And naturally, when they grow up, they helplessly exchange the prison of the school for the prison of the mine or the workshop or the office, and drudge along stupidly and miserably, with just enough gregarious instinct to turn furiously on any intelligent person who proposes a change. It would be quite easy to make England a paradise, according to our present ideas, in a few years. There is no mystery about it: the way has been pointed out over and over again. The difficulty is not the way but the will. And we have no will because the first thing done with us in childhood was to break our will. Can anything be more disgusting than the spectacle of a nation reading the biography of Gladstone and gloating over the account of how he was flogged at Eton, two of his schoolfellows being compelled to hold him down whilst he was flogged. Not long ago a public body in England had to deal with the case of a schoolmaster who, conceiving himself insulted by the smoking of a cigaret against his orders by a pupil eighteen years old, proposed to flog him publicly as a satisfaction to what he called his honor and authority. I had intended to give the particulars of this case, but find the drudgery of raking over such stuff too sickening, and the effect unjust to a man who was doing only what others all over the country were doing as part of the established routine of what is called education. The astounding part of it was the manner in which the person to whom this outrage on decency seemed quite proper and natural claimed to be a functionary of high character, and had his claim allowed. In Japan he would hardly have been allowed the privilege of committing suicide. What is to be said of a profession in which such obscenities are made points of honor, or of institutions in which they are an accepted part of the daily routine? Wholesome people would not argue about the taste of such nastinesses: they would spit them out; but we are tainted with flagellomania from our childhood. When will we realize that the fact that we can become accustomed to anything, however disgusting at first, makes it necessary for us to examine carefully everything we have become accustomed to? Before motor cars became common, necessity had accustomed us to a foulness in our streets which would have horrified us had the street been our drawingroom carpet. Before long we shall be as particular about our streets as we now are about our carpets; and their condition in the nineteenth century will become as forgotten and incredible as the condition of the corridors of palaces and the courts of castles was as late as the eighteenth century. This foulness, we can plead, was imposed on us as a necessity by the use of horses and of huge retinues; but flogging has never been so imposed: it has always been a vice, craved for on any pretext by those depraved by it. Boys were flogged when criminals were hanged, to impress the awful warning on them. Boys were flogged at boundaries, to impress the boundaries on their memory. Other methods and other punishments were always available: the choice of this one betrayed the sensual impulse which makes the practice an abomination. But when its viciousness made it customary, it was practised and tolerated on all hands by people who were innocent of anything worse than stupidity, ill temper, and inability to discover other methods of maintaining order than those they had always seen practised and approved of. From children and animals it extended to slaves and criminals. In the days of Moses it was limited to 39 lashes. In the early nineteenth century it had become an open madness: soldiers were sentenced to a thousand lashes for trifling offences, with the result (among others less mentionable) that the Iron Duke of Wellington complained that it was impossible to get an order obeyed in the British army except in two or three crack regiments. Such frantic excesses of this disgusting neurosis provoked a reaction against it; but the clamor for it by depraved persons never ceased, and was tolerated by a nation trained to it from childhood in the schools until last year

(1913), when, in what must be described as a paroxysm of sexual excitement provoked by the agitation concerning the White Slave Traffic (the purely commercial nature of which I was prevented from exposing on the stage by the Censorship twenty years ago), the Government yielded to an outcry for flagellation led by the Archbishop of Canterbury, and passed an Act under which a judge can sentence a man to be flogged to the utmost extremity with any instrument usable for such a purpose that he cares to prescribe. Such an Act is not a legislative phenomenon but a psychopathic one. Its effect on the White Slave Traffic was, of course, to distract public attention from its real cause and from the people who really profit by it to imaginary "foreign scoundrels," and to secure a monopoly of its organization for women.

And all this evil is made possible by the schoolmaster with his cane and birch, by the parents getting rid as best they can of the nuisance of children making noise and mischief in the house, and by the denial to children of the elementary rights of human beings.

The first man who enslaved and "broke in" an animal with a whip would have invented the explosion engine instead could he have foreseen the curse he was laying on his race. For men and women learnt thereby to enslave and break in their children by the same means. These children, grown up, knew no other methods of training. Finally the evil that was done for gain by the greedy was refined on and done for pleasure by the lustful. Flogging has become a pleasure purchasable in our streets, and inhibition a grown-up habit that children play at. "Go and see what baby is doing; and tell him he mustnt" is the last word of the nursery; and the grimmest aspect of it is that it was first formulated by a comic paper as a capital joke.

TECHNICAL INSTRUCTION

Technical instruction tempts to violence (as a short cut) more than liberal education. The sailor in Mr Rudyard

Kipling's Captains Courageous, teaching the boy the names of the ship's tackle with a rope's end, does not disgust us as our schoolmasters do, especially as the boy was a spoiled boy. But an unspoiled boy would not have needed that drastic medicine. Technical training may be as tedious as learning to skate or to play the piano or violin; but it is the price one must pay to achieve certain desirable results or necessary ends. It is a monstrous thing to force a child to learn Latin or Greek or mathematics on the ground that they are an indispensable gymnastic for the mental powers. It would be monstrous even if it were true; for there is no labor that might not be imposed on a child or an adult on the same pretext; but as a glance at the average products of our public school and university education shews that it is not true, it need not trouble us. But it is a fact that ignorance of Latin and Greek and mathematics closes certain careers to men (I do not mean artificial, unnecessary, noxious careers like those of the commercial schoolmaster). Languages, even dead ones, have their uses; and, as it seems to many of us, mathematics have their uses. They will always be learned by people who want to learn them; and people will always want to learn them as long as they are of any importance in life: indeed the want will survive their importance: superstition is nowhere stronger than in the field of obsolete acquirements. And they will never be learnt fruitfully by people who do not want to learn them either for their own sake or for use in necessary work. There is no harder schoolmaster than experience; and yet experience fails to teach where there is no desire to learn.

Still, one must not begin to apply this generalization too early. And this brings me to an important factor in the case: the factor of evolution.

DOCILITY AND DEPENDENCE

If anyone, impressed by my view that the rights of a child are precisely those of an adult, proceeds to treat a child as if it were an adult, he (or she) will find that though the plan will work much better at some points than the usual plan, at others it will not work at all; and this discovery may provoke him to turn back from the whole conception of children's rights with a jest at the expense of bachelors' and old maids' children. In dealing with children what is needed is not logic but sense. There is no logical reason why young persons should be allowed greater control of their property the day after they are twenty-one than the day before it. There is no logical reason why I, who strongly object to an adult standing over a boy of ten with a Latin grammar, and saying "You must learn this, whether you want to or not," should nevertheless be quite prepared to stand over a boy of five with the multiplication table or a copy book or a code of elementary good manners, and practise on his docility to make him learn them. And there is no logical reason why I should do for a child a great many little offices, some of them troublesome and disagreeable, which I should not do for a boy twice its age, or support a boy or girl when I would unhesitatingly throw an adult on his own resources. But there are practical reasons, and sensible reasons, and affectionate reasons for all these illogicalities. Children do not want to be treated altogether as adults: such treatment terrifies them and overburdens them with responsibility. In truth, very few adults care to be called on for independence and originality: they also are bewildered and terrified in the absence of precedents and precepts and commandments; but modern Democracy allows them a sanctioning and cancelling power if they are capable of using it, which children are not. To treat a child wholly as an adult would be to mock and destroy it. Infantile docility and juvenile dependence are, like death, a product of Natural Selection; and though there is no viler crime than to abuse them, yet there is no greater cruelty than to ignore them. I have complained sufficiently of what I suffered through the process of assault, imprisonment, and compulsory lessons that taught me nothing, which are called my schooling. But I could say a good deal also about the things I was not taught and should have been taught, not to mention the things I was allowed to do which I should not have been allowed to do. I have no recollection of being taught to read or write; so I presume I was born with both faculties; but many people seem to have bitter recollections of being forced reluctantly to acquire them. And though I have the uttermost contempt for a teacher so ill-mannered and incompetent as to be unable to make a child learn to read and write without also making it 'cry, still I am prepared to admit that I had rather have been compelled to learn to read and write with tears by an incompetent and ill-mannered person than left in ignorance. Reading, writing, and enough arithmetic to use money honestly and accurately, together with the rudiments of law and order, become necessary conditions of a child's liberty before it can appreciate the importance of its liberty, or foresee that these accomplishments are worth acquiring. Nature has provided for this by evolving the instinct of docility. Children are very docile: they have a sound intuition that they must do what they are told or perish. And adults have an intuition, equally sound, that they must take advantage of this docility to teach children how to live properly or the children will not survive. The difficulty is to know where to stop. To illustrate this, let us consider the main danger of childish docility and parental officiousness.

THE ABUSE OF DOCILITY

Docility may survive as a lazy habit long after it has ceased to be a beneficial instinct. If you catch a child when it is young enough to be instinctively docile, and keep it in a condition of unremitted tutelage under the nurserymaid, the governess, the preparatory school, the secondary school, and the university, until it is an adult, you will produce, not a self-reliant, free, fully matured

human being, but a grown-up schoolboy or schoolgirl,
capable of nothing in the way of original or independent
action except outbursts of naughtiness in the women and
blackguardism in the men. That is exactly what we get
at present in our rich and consequently governing classes:
they pass from juvenility to senility without ever touch-
ing maturity except in body. The classes which cannot
afford this sustained tutelage are notably more self-reliant
and grown-up: an office boy of fifteen is often more of a
man than a university student of twenty. Unfortunately
this precocity is disabled by poverty, ignorance, narrow-
ness, and a hideous power of living without art or love or
beauty and being rather proud of it. The poor never
escape from servitude: their docility is preserved by their
slavery. And so all become the prey of the greedy, the
selfish, the domineering, the unscrupulous, the predatory.
If here and there an individual refuses to be docile, ten
docile persons will beat him or lock him up or shoot him
or hang him at the bidding of his oppressors and their
own. The crux of the whole difficulty about parents,
schoolmasters, priests, absolute monarchs, and despots of
every sort, is the tendency to abuse natural docility. A
nation should always be healthily rebellious; but rulers
have yet to be found who will make trouble for themselves
by cultivating that side of the national spirit. A child should
begin to assert itself early, and shift for itself more and
more not only in washing and dressing itself, but in opinions and conduct; yet as nothing is so exasperating and
so unlovable as an uppish child, it is useless to expect
parents and schoolmasters to inculcate this uppishness.
Such unamiable precepts as Always contradict an author-
itative statement, Always return a blow, Never lose a
chance of a good fight, When you are scolded for a mistake ask the person who scolds you whether he or she sup-
poses you did it on purpose, and follow the question with
a blow or an insult or some other unmistakeable expression
of resentment, Remember that the progress of the world
depends on your knowing better than your elders, are just

as important as those of the sermon on the mount; but no one has yet seen them written up in letters of gold in a schoolroom or nursery. The child is taught to be kind, to be respectful, to be quiet, not to answer back, to be truthful when its elders want to find out anything from it, to lie when the truth would shock or hurt its elders, to be above all things obedient, and to be seen and not heard. Here we have two sets of precepts, each of which will spoil an ordinary child if the other be omitted. Unfortunately we do not allow fair play between them. The rebellious, intractable, aggressive, selfish set provoke a corrective resistance, and do not pretend to high moral or religious sanctions; and they are never urged by grown-up people on young people. They are therefore more in danger of neglect or suppression than the other set, which have all the adults, all the laws, all the religions on their side. How is the child to be secured its due share of both bodies of doctrine?

THE SCHOOLBOY AND THE HOMEBOY

In practice what happens is that parents notice that boys brought up at home become mollycoddles, or prigs, or duffers, unable to take care of themselves. They see that boys should learn to rough it a little and to mix with children of their own age. This is natural enough. When you have preached at and punished a boy until he is a moral cripple, you are as much hampered by him as by a physical cripple; and as you do not intend to have him on your hands all your life, and are generally rather impatient for the day when he will earn his own living and leave you to attend to yourself, you sooner or later begin to talk to him about the need for self-reliance, learning to think, and so forth, with the result that your victim, bewildered by your inconsistency, concludes that there is no use trying to please you, and falls into an attitude of sulky resentment. Which is an additional inducement to pack him off to school.

In school, he finds himself in a dual world, under two dispensations. There is the world of the boys, where the point of honor is to be untameable, always ready to fight, ruthless in taking the conceit out of anyone who ventures to give himself airs of superior knowledge or taste, and generally to take Lucifer for one's model. And there is the world of the masters, the world of discipline, submission, diligence, obedience, and continual and shameless assumption of moral and intellectual authority. Thus the schoolboy hears both sides, and is so far better off than the homebred boy who hears only one. But the two sides are not fairly presented. They are presented as good and evil, as vice and virtue, as villainy and heroism. The boy feels mean and cowardly when he obeys, and selfish and rascally when he disobeys. He loses his moral courage just as he comes to hate books and languages. In the end, John Ruskin, tied so closely to his mother's apron-string that he did not escape even when he went to Oxford, and John Stuart Mill, whose father ought to have been prosecuted for laying his son's childhood waste with lessons, were superior, as products of training, to our schoolboys. They were very conspicuously superior in moral courage; and though they did not distinguish themselves at cricket and football, they had quite as much physical hardihood as any civilized man needs. But it is to be observed that Ruskin's parents were wise people who gave John a full share in their own life, and put up with his presence both at home and abroad when they must sometimes have been very weary of him; and Mill, as it happens, was deliberately educated to challenge all the most sacred institutions of his country. The households they were brought up in were no more average households than a Montessori school is an average school.

THE COMINGS OF AGE OF CHILDREN

All this inculcated adult docility, which wrecks every civilization as it is wrecking ours, is inhuman and unnatural. We must reconsider our institution of the Coming of Age, which is too late for some purposes, and too early for others. There should be a series of Coming of Ages for every individual. The mammals have their first coming of age when they are weaned; and it is noteworthy that this rather cruel and selfish operation on the part of the parent has to be performed resolutely, with claws and teeth; for your little mammal does not want to be weaned, and yields only to a pretty rough assertion of the right of the parent to be relieved of the child as soon as the child is old enough to bear the separation. The same thing occurs with children: they hang on to the mother's apron-string and the father's coat tails as long as they can, often baffling those sensitive parents who know that children should think for themselves and fend for themselves, but are too kind to throw them on their own resources with the ferocity of the domestic cat. The child should have its first coming of age when it is weaned, another when it can talk, another when it can walk, another when it can dress itself without assistance; and when it can read, write, count money, and pass an examination in going a simple errand involving a purchase and a journey by rail or other public method of locomotion, it should have quite a majority. At present the children of laborers are soon mobile and able to shift for themselves, whereas it is possible to find grown-up women in the rich classes who are actually afraid to take a walk in the streets unattended and unprotected. It is true that this is a superstition from the time when a retinue was part of the state of persons of quality, and the unattended person was supposed to be a common person of no quality, earning a living; but this has now become so absurd that children and young women are no longer told why they are forbidden to go about alone, and have to be persuaded that the streets are dangerous places, which of course they are; but people who are not educated to live dangerously have only half a life, and are more likely to die miserably after all than those who have taken all the common risks of freedom from their childhood onward as matters of course.

THE CONFLICT OF WILLS

The world wags in spite of its schools and its families because both schools and families are mostly very largely anarchic: parents and schoolmasters are goodnatured or weak or lazy; and children are docile and affectionate and very shortwinded in their fits of naughtiness; and so most families slummock along and muddle through until the children cease to be children. In the few cases when the parties are energetic and determined, the child is crushed or the parent is reduced to a cipher, as the case may be. When the opposed forces are neither of them strong enough to annihilate the other, there is serious trouble: that is how we get those feuds between parent and child which recur to our memory so ironically when we hear people sentimentalizing about natural affection. We even get tragedies; for there is nothing so tragic to contemplate or so devastating to suffer as the oppression of will without conscience; and the whole tendency of our family and school system is to set the will of the parent and the school despot above conscience as something that must be deferred to abjectly and absolutely for its own sake.

The strongest, fiercest force in nature is human will. It is the highest organization we know of the will that has created the whole universe. Now all honest civilization, religion, law, and convention is an attempt to keep this force within beneficent bounds. What corrupts civilization, religion, law, and convention (and they are at present pretty nearly as corrupt as they dare) is the constant attempts made by the wills of individuals and classes to thwart the wills and enslave the powers of other individuals and classes. The powers of the parent and the schoolmaster, and of their public analogues the lawgiver and the judge, become instruments of tyranny in the hands of those who are too narrow-minded to understand law and exercise judgment; and in their hands (with us they mostly fall into such hands) law becomes tyranny. And what is a tyrant? Quite simply a person who says to another person, young or old, "You shall do as I tell you; you shall make what I want; you shall profess my creed; you shall have no will of your own; and your powers shall be at the disposal of my will." It has come to this at last: that the phrase "she has a will of her own," or "he has a will of his own" has come to denote a person of exceptional obstinacy and self-assertion. And even persons of good natural disposition, if brought up to expect such deference, are roused to unreasoning fury, and sometimes to the commission of atrocious crimes, by the slightest challenge to their authority. Thus a laborer may be dirty, drunken, untruthful, slothful, untrustworthy in every way without exhausting the indulgence of the country-house. But let him dare to be "disrespectful" and he is a lost man, though he be the cleanest, soberest, most diligent, most veracious, most trustworthy man in the county. Dickens's instinct for detecting social cankers never served him better than when he shewed up Mrs Heep teaching her son to "be umble," knowing that if he carried out that precept he might be pretty well anything else he liked. The maintenance of deference to our wills becomes a mania which will carry the best of us to any extremity. We will allow a village of Egyptian fellaheen or Indian tribesmen to live the lowest life they please among themselves without molestation; but let one of them slay an Englishman or even strike him on the strongest provocation, and straightway we go stark mad, burning and destroying, shooting and shelling, flogging and hanging, if only such survivors as we may leave are thoroughly cowed in the presence of a man with a white face. In the committee room of a local council or city corporation, the humblest employees of the committee find defenders if they complain of harsh treatment. Gratuities are voted, indulgences and holidays are pleaded for, delinquencies are excused in the most sentimental manner provided only the employee, however patent a hypocrite or incorrigible a slacker, is hat in hand. But let the most obvious measure of justice be demanded by the secretary of a Trade Union in terms which omit all expressions of subservience, and it is with the greatest difficulty that the cooler-headed can defeat angry motions that the letter be thrown into the waste-paper basket and the committee proceed to the next business.

THE DEMAGOGUE'S OPPORTUNITY

And the employee has in him the same fierce impulse to impose his will without respect for the will of others. Democracy is in practice nothing but a device for cajoling from him the vote he refuses to arbitrary authority. He will not vote for Coriolanus; but when an experienced demagogue comes along and says "Sir: *you* are the dictator: the voice of the people is the voice of God; and I am only your very humble servant" he says at once "All right: tell me what to dictate" and is presently enslaved more effectually with his own silly consent than Coriolanus would ever have enslaved him without asking his leave. And the trick by which the demagogue defeats Coriolanus is played on him in his turn by *his* inferiors. Everywhere we see the cunning succeeding in the world by seeking a rich or powerful master and practising on his lust for subservience. The political adventurer who gets into parliament by offering himself to the poor voter, not as his representative but as his will-less soulless "delegate," is himself the dupe of a clever wife who repudiates Votes for Women, knowing well that whilst the man is master, the man's mistress will rule. Uriah Heep may be a crawling creature; but his crawling takes him upstairs.

Thus does the selfishness of the will turn on itself, and obtain by flattery what it cannot seize by open force. Democracy becomes the latest trick of tyranny: "womanliness" becomes the latest wile of prostitution.

Between parent and child the same conflict wages and

the same destruction of character ensues. Parents set themselves to bend the will of their children to their own —to break their stubborn spirit, as they call it—with the ruthlessness of Grand Inquisitors. Cunning, unscrupulous children learn all the arts of the sneak in circumventing tyranny: children of better character are cruelly distressed and more or less lamed for life by it.

OUR QUARRELSOMENESS

As between adults, we find a general quarrelsomeness which makes political reform as impossible to most Englishmen as to hogs. Certain sections of the nation get cured of this disability. University men, sailors, and politicians are comparatively free from it, because the communal life of the university, the fact that in a ship a man must either learn to consider others or else go overboard or into irons, and the habit of working on committees and ceasing to expect more of one's own way than is included in the greatest common measure of the committee, educate the will socially. But no one who has ever had to guide a committee of ordinary private English-men through their first attempts at collective action, in committee or otherwise, can retain any illusions as to the appalling effects on our national manners and character of the organization of the home and the school as petty tyrannies, and the absence of all teaching of self-respect and training in self-assertion. Bullied and ordered about, the Englishman obeys like a sheep, evades like a knave, or tries to murder his oppressor. Merely criticized or op-posed in committee, or invited to consider anybody's views but his own, he feels personally insulted and wants to resign or leave the room unless he is apologized to. And his panic and bewilderment when he sees that the older hands at the work have no patience with him and do not intend to treat him as infallible, are pitiable as far as they are anything but ludicrous. That is what comes of not being taught to consider other people's wills, and left to submit to them or to override them as if they were the winds and the weather. Such a state of mind is incompatible not only with the democratic introduction of high civilization, but with the comprehension and maintenance of such civilized institutions as have been introduced by benevolent and intelligent despots and aristocrats.

WE MUST REFORM SOCIETY BEFORE WE CAN REFORM OURSELVES

When we come to the positive problem of what to do with children if we are to give up the established plan, we find the difficulties so great that we begin to understand why so many people who detest the system and look back with loathing on their own schooldays, must helplessly send their children to the very schools they themselves were sent to, because there is no alternative except abandoning the children to undisciplined vagabondism. Man in society must do as everybody else does in his class: only fools and romantic novices imagine that freedom is a mere matter of the readiness of the individual to snap his fingers at convention. It is true that most of us live in a condition of quite unnecessary inhibition, wearing ugly and uncomfortable clothes, making ourselves and other people miserable by the heathen horrors of mourning, staying away from the theatre because we cannot afford the stalls and are ashamed to go to the pit, and in dozens of other ways enslaving ourselves when there are comfortable alternatives open to us without any real drawbacks. The contemplation of these petty slaveries, and of the triumphant ease with which sensible people throw them off, creates an impression that if we only take Johnson's advice to free our minds from cant, we can achieve freedom. But if we all freed our minds from cant we should find that for the most part we should have to go on doing the necessary work of the world exactly as we did it before until we organized new and free methods of doing it. Many people believed in secondary co-educa-

tion (boys and girls taught together) before schools like
Bedales were founded: indeed the practice was common
enough in elementary schools and in Scotland; but their
belief did not help them until Bedales and St George's
were organized; and there are still not nearly enough co-
educational schools in existence to accommodate all the
children of the parents who believe in co-education up to
university age, even if they could always afford the fees
of these exceptional schools. It may be edifying to tell
a duke that our public schools are all wrong in their constitution and methods, or a costermonger that children
should be treated as in Goethe's Wilhelm Meister instead
of as they are treated at the elementary school at the
corner of his street; but what are the duke and the coster
to do? Neither of them has any effective choice in the
matter: their children must either go to the schools that
are, or to no school at all. And as the duke thinks with
reason that his son will be a lout or a milksop or a prig
if he does not go to school, and the coster knows that his
son will become an illiterate hooligan if he is left to the
streets, there is no real alternative for either of them.
Child life must be socially organized: no parent, rich or
poor, can choose institutions that do not exist; and the
private enterprise of individual schoolmasters appealing
to a group of well-to-do parents, though it may shew what
can be done by enthusiasts with new methods, cannot
touch the mass of our children. For the average parent
or child nothing is really available except the established
practice; and this is what makes it so important that the
established practice should be a sound one, and so useless for clever individuals to disparage it unless they can
organize an alternative practice and make it, too, general.

THE PURSUIT OF MANNERS

If you cross-examine the duke and the coster, you will
find that they are not concerned for the scholastic attain-
ments of their children. Ask the duke whether he could

pass the standard examination of twelve-year-old children in elementary schools, and he will admit, with an entirely placid smile, that he would almost certainly be ignominiously plucked. And he is so little ashamed of or disadvantaged by his condition that he is not prepared to spend an hour in remedying it. The coster may resent the inquiry instead of being amused by it; but his answer, if true, will be the same. What they both want for their children is the communal training, the apprenticeship to society, the lessons in holding one's own among people of all sorts with whom one is not, as in the home, on privileged terms. These can be acquired only by "mixing with the world," no matter how wicked the world is. No parent cares twopence whether his children can write Latin hexameters or repeat the dates of the accession of all the English monarchs since the Conqueror; but all parents are earnestly anxious about the manners of their children. Better Claude Duval than Kaspar Hauser. Laborers who are contemptuously anti-clerical in their opinions will send their daughters to the convent school because the nuns teach them some sort of gentleness of speech and behavior. And peers who tell you that our public schools are rotten through and through, and that our universities ought to be razed to the foundations, send their sons to Eton and Oxford, Harrow and Cambridge, not only because there is nothing else to be done, but because these places, though they turn out blackguards and ignoramuses and boobies galore, turn them out with the habits and manners of the society they belong to. Bad as those manners are in many respects, they are better than no manners at all. And no individual or family can possibly teach them. They can be acquired only by living in an organized community in which they are traditional.

Thus we see that there are reasons for the segregation of children even in families where the great reason: namely, that children are nuisances to adults, does not press very hardly, as, for instance, in the houses of the very poor, who can send their children to play in the streets, or the houses of the very rich, which are so large that the children's quarters can be kept out of the parents' way like the servants' quarters.

NOT TOO MUCH WIND ON THE HEATH, BROTHER

What, then, is to be done? For the present, unfortunately, little except propagating the conception of Children's Rights. Only the achievement of economic equality through Socialism can make it possible to deal thoroughly with the question from the point of view of the total interest of the community, which must always consist of grown-up children. Yet economic equality, like all simple and obvious arrangements, seems impossible to people brought up as children are now. Still, something can be done even within class limits. Large communities of children of the same class are possible today; and voluntary organization of outdoor life for children has already begun in Boy Scouting and excursions of one kind or another. The discovery that anything, even school life, is better for the child than home life, will become an overridden hobby; and we shall presently be told by our faddists that anything, even camp life, is better than school life. Some blundering beginnings of this are already perceptible. There is a movement for making our British children into priggish little barefooted vagabonds, all talking like that born fool George Borrow, and supposed to be splendidly healthy because they would die if they slept in rooms with the windows shut, or perhaps even with a roof over their heads. Still, this is a fairly healthy folly; and it may do something to establish Mr Harold Cox's claim of a Right to Roam as the basis of a much needed law compelling proprietors of land to provide plenty of gates in their fences, and to leave them unlocked when there are no growing crops to be damaged nor bulls to be encountered, instead of, as at present, imprisoning the human race in dusty or muddy thoroughfares between walls of barbed wire.

The reaction against vagabondage will come from the children themselves. For them freedom will not mean the expensive kind of savagery now called "the simple life." Their natural disgust with the visions of cockney book fanciers blowing themselves out with "the wind on the heath, brother," and of anarchists who are either too weak to understand that men are strong and free in proportion to the social pressure they can stand and the complexity of the obligations they are prepared to undertake, or too strong to realize that what is freedom to them may be terror and bewilderment to others, will drive them back to the home and the school if these have meanwhile learned the lesson that children are independent human beings and have rights.

WANTED: A CHILD'S MAGNA CHARTA

Whether we shall presently be discussing a Juvenile Magna Charta or Declaration of Rights by way of including children in the Constitution is a question on which I leave others to speculate. But if it could once be established that a child has an adult's Right of Egress from uncomfortable places and unpleasant company, and there were children's lawyers to sue pedagogues and others for assault and imprisonment, there would be an amazing change in the behavior of schoolmasters, the quality of school books, and the amenities of school life. That Consciousness of Consent which, even in its present delusive form, has enabled Democracy to oust tyrannical systems in spite of all its vulgarities and stupidities and rancors and ineptitudes and ignorances, would operate as powerfully among children as it does now among grown-ups. No doubt the pedagogue would promptly turn demagogue, and woo his scholars by all the arts of demagogy; but none of these arts can easily be so dishonorable or mischievous as the art of caning. And, after all, if larger liberties are attached to the acquisition of knowledge, and the child finds that it can no more go to the seaside with-

out a knowledge of the multiplication and pence tables
than it can be an astronomer without mathematics, it will
learn the multiplication table, which is more than it always
does at present, in spite of all the canings and keep-
ings-in.

THE PURSUIT OF LEARNING

When the Pursuit of Learning comes to mean the pursuit
of learning by the child instead of the pursuit of the child
by Learning, cane in hand, the danger will be precocity
of the intellect, which is just as undesirable as precocity
of the emotions. We still have a silly habit of talking and
thinking as if intellect were a mechanical process and not
a passion; and in spite of the German tutors who confess openly that three out of every five of the young men
they coach for examinations are lamed for life thereby;
in spite of Dickens and his picture of little Paul Dombey
dying of lessons, we persist in heaping on growing children
and adolescent youths and maidens tasks Pythagoras
would have declined out of common regard for his own
health and common modesty as to his own capacity. And
this overwork is not all the effect of compulsion; for the
average schoolmaster does not compel his scholars to
learn; he only scolds and punishes them if they do not,
which is quite a different thing, the net effect being that
the school prisoners need not learn unless they like. Nay,
it is sometimes remarked that the school dunce—meaning
the one who does not like—often turns out well afterwards, as if idleness were a sign of ability and character.
A much more sensible explanation is that the so-called
dunces are not exhausted before they begin the serious
business of life. It is said that boys will be boys; and one
can only add one wishes they would. Boys really want to
be manly, and are unfortunately encouraged thoughtlessly
in this very dangerous and overstraining aspiration. All
the people who have really worked (Herbert Spencer for
instance) warn us against work as earnestly as some peo-

ple warn us against drink. When learning is placed on the voluntary footing of sport, the teacher will find himself saying every day "Run away and play: you have worked as much as is good for you." Trying to make children leave school will be like trying to make them go to bed; and it will be necessary to surprise them with the idea that teaching is work, and that the teacher is tired and must go play or rest or eat: possibilities always concealed by that infamous humbug the current schoolmaster, who achieves a spurious divinity and a witch doctor's authority by persuading children that he is not human, just as ladies used to persuade them that they have no legs.

CHILDREN AND GAME: A PROPOSAL

Of the many wild absurdities of our existing social order perhaps the most grotesque is the costly and strictly enforced reservation of large tracts of country as deer forests and breeding grounds for pheasants whilst there is so little provision of the kind made for children. I have more than once thought of trying to introduce the shooting of children as a sport, as the children would then be preserved very carefully for ten months in the year, thereby reducing their death rate far more than the fusillades of the sportsmen during the other two would raise it. At present the killing of a fox except by a pack of foxhounds is regarded with horror; but you may and do kill children in a hundred and fifty ways provided you do not shoot them or set a pack of dogs on them. It must be admitted that the foxes have the best of it; and indeed a glance at our pheasants, our deer, and our children will convince the most sceptical that the children have decidedly the worst of it.

This much hope, however, can be extracted from the present state of things. It is so fantastic, so mad, so apparently impossible, that no scheme of reform need ever henceforth be discredited on the ground that it is fantastic or mad or apparently impossible. It is the sensible schemes, unfortunately, that are hopeless in England. Therefore I have great hopes that my own views, though fundamentally sensible, can be made to appear fantastic enough to have a chance.

First, then, I lay it down as a prime condition of sane society, obvious as such to anyone but an idiot, that in any decent community, children should find in every part of their native country, food, clothing, lodging, instruction, and parental kindness for the asking. For the matter of that, so should adults; but the two cases differ in that as these commodities do not grow on the bushes, the adults cannot have them unless they themselves organize and provide the supply, whereas the children must have them as if by magic, with nothing to do but rub the lamp, like Aladdin, and have their needs satisfied.

THE PARENTS' INTOLERABLE BURDEN

There is nothing new in this: it is how children have always had and must always have their needs satisfied. The parent has to play the part of Aladdin's djinn; and many a parent has sunk beneath the burden of this service. All the novelty we need is to organize it so that instead of the individual child fastening like a parasite on its own particular parents, the whole body of children should be thrown not only upon the whole body of parents, but upon the celibates and childless as well, whose present exemption from a full share in the social burden of children is obviously unjust and unwholesome. Today it is easy to find a widow who has at great cost to herself in pain, danger, and disablement, borne six or eight children. In the same town you will find rich bachelors and old maids, and married couples with no children or with families voluntarily limited to two or three. The eight children do not belong to the woman in any real or legal sense. When she has reared them they pass away from her into the community as independent persons, marrying strangers, working for strangers, spending on the community the life that has been built up at her expense. No more monstrous injustice could be imagined than that the burden of rearing the children should fall on her alone and not on the celibates and the selfish as well.

This is so far recognized that already the child finds, wherever is goes, a school for it, and somebody to force it into the school; and more and more these schools are being driven by the mere logic of facts to provide the children with meals, with boots, with spectacles, with dentists and doctors. In fact, when the child's parents are destitute or not to be found, bread, lodging, and clothing are provided. It is true that they are provided grudgingly and on conditions infamous enough to draw down abundant fire from Heaven upon us every day in the shape of crime and disease and vice; but still the practice of keeping children barely alive at the charge of the community is established; and there is no need for me to argue about it. I propose only two extensions of the practice. One is to provide for all the child's reasonable human wants, on which point, if you differ from me, I shall take leave to say that you are socially a fool and personally an inhuman wretch. The other is that these wants should be supplied in complete freedom from compulsory schooling or compulsory anything except restraint from crime, though, as they can be supplied only by social organization, the child must be conscious of and subject to the conditions of that organization, which may involve such portions of adult responsibility and duty as a child may be able to bear according to its age, and which will in any case prevent it from forming the vagabond and anarchist habit of mind.

One more exception might be necessary: compulsory freedom. I am sure that a child should not be imprisoned in a school. I am not so sure that it should not sometimes be driven out into the open—imprisoned in the woods and on the mountains, as it were. For there are frowsty children, just as there are frowsty adults, who dont want freedom. This morbid result of over-domestication would, let us hope, soon disappear with its cause.

Those who see no prospect held out to them by this except a country in which all the children shall be roaming savages, should consider, first, whether their condition would be any worse than that of the little caged savages of today; and second, whether either children or adults are so apt to run wild that it is necessary to tether them fast to one neighborhood to prevent a general dissolution of society. My own observation leads me to believe that we are not half mobilized enough. True, I cannot deny that we are more mobile than we were. You will still find in the home counties old men who have never been to London, and who tell you that they once went to Winchester or St Albans much as if they had been to the South Pole; but they are not so common as the clerk who has been to Paris or to Lovely Lucerne, and who "goes away somewhere" when he has a holiday. His grandfather never had a holiday, and, if he had, would no more have dreamed of crossing the Channel than of taking a box at the Opera. But with all allowance for the Polytechnic excursion and the tourist agency, our inertia is still appalling. I confess to having once spent nine years in London without putting my nose outside it; and though this was better, perhaps, than the restless globetrotting vagabondage of the idle rich, wandering from hotel to hotel and never really living anywhere, yet I should no more have done it if I had been properly mobilized in my childhood than I should have worn the same suit of clothes all that time (which, by the way, I very nearly did, my professional income not having as yet begun to sprout). There are masses of people who could afford at least a trip to Margate, and a good many who could afford a trip round the world, who are more immovable than Aldgate pump. To others, who would move if they knew how, travelling is surrounded with imaginary difficulties and terrors. In short, the difficulty is not to fix people, but to root them up. We keep repeating the silly proverb that a rolling stone gathers no moss, as if moss were a desirable parasite. What we mean is that a vagabond does not prosper. Even this is not true, if prosperity means enjoyment as well as responsibility and money. The real misery of vagabondage is the misery of having nothing to do and nowhere to go, the misery of being derelict of God and Man, the misery of the idle, poor or rich. And this is one of the miseries of unoccupied childhood. The unoccupied adult, thus afflicted, tries many distractions which are, to say the least, unsuited to children. But one of them, the distraction of seeing the world, is innocent and beneficial. Also it is childish, being a continuation of what nurses call "taking notice," by which a child becomes experienced. It is pitiable nowadays to see men and women doing after the age of 45 all the travelling and sightseeing they should have done before they were 15. Mere wondering and staring at things is an important part of a child's education: that is why children can be thoroughly mobilized without making vagabonds of them. A vagabond is at home nowhere because he wanders: a child should wander because it ought to be at home everywhere. And if it has its papers and its passports, and gets what it requires not by begging and pilfering, but from responsible agents of the community as of right, and with some formal acknowledgment of the obligations it is incurring and a knowledge of the fact that these obligations are being recorded: if, further, certain qualifications are exacted before it is promoted from permission to go as far as its legs will carry it to using mechanical aids to locomotion, it can roam without much danger of gypsification.

Under such circumstances the boy or girl could always run away, and never be lost; and on no other conditions can a child be free without being also a homeless outcast. Parents could also run away from disagreeable children or drive them out of doors or even drop their acquaintance, temporarily or permanently, without inhumanity. Thus both parties would be on their good behavior, and not, as at present, on their filial or parental behavior, which, like all unfree behavior, is mostly bad behavior.

As to what other results might follow, we had better wait and see; for nobody now alive can imagine what customs and institutions would grow up in societies of free children. Child laws and child fashions, child manners and child morals are now not tolerated; but among free children there would certainly be surprising developments in this direction. I do not think there would be any danger of free children behaving as badly as grown-up people do now because they have never been free. They could hardly behave worse, anyhow.

CHILDREN'S RIGHTS AND PARENTS' WRONGS

A very distinguished man once assured a mother of my acquaintance that she would never know what it meant to be hurt until she was hurt through her children. Children are extremely cruel without intending it; and in ninety-nine cases out of a hundred the reason is that they do not conceive their elders as having any human feelings. Serve the elders right, perhaps, for posing as superhuman! The penalty of the impostor is not that he is found out (he very seldom is) but that he is taken for what he pretends to be, and treated as such. And to be treated as anything but what you really are may seem pleasant to the imagination when the treatment is above your merits; but in actual experience it is often quite the reverse. When I was a very small boy, my romantic imagination, stimulated by early doses of fiction, led me to brag to a still smaller boy so outrageously that he, being a simple soul, really believed me to be an invincible hero. I cannot remember whether this pleased me much; but I do remember very distinctly that one day this admirer of mine, who had a pet goat, found the animal in the hands of a larger boy than either of us, who mocked him and refused to restore the animal to his rightful owner. Whereupon, naturally, he came weeping to me, and demanded that I should rescue the goat and annihilate the aggressor. My terror was beyond description: fortunately for me, it imparted such a ghastliness to my voice and aspect as I, under the eye of my poor little dupe, advanced on the enemy with that hideous extremity of cowardice which is called the courage of despair, and said "You let go that goat," that he abandoned his prey and fled, to my unforgettable, unspeakable relief. I have never since exaggerated my prowess in bodily combat.

Now what happened to me in the adventure of the goat happens very often to parents, and would happen to schoolmasters if the prison door of the school did not shut out the trials of life. I remember once, at school, the resident head master was brought down to earth by the sudden illness of his wife. In the confusion that ensued it became necessary to leave one of the schoolrooms without a master. I was in the class that occupied that schoolroom. To have sent us home would have been to break the fundamental bargain with our parents by which the school was bound to keep us out of their way for half the day at all hazards. Therefore an appeal had to be made to out better feelings: that is, to our common humanity, not to make a noise. But the head master had never admitted any common humanity with us. We had been carefully broken in to regard him as a being quite aloof from and above us: one not subject to error or suffering or death or illness or mortality. Consequently sympathy was impossible; and if the unfortunate lady did not perish, it was because, as I now comfort myself with guessing, she was too much preoccupied with her own pains, and possibly making too much noise herself, to be conscious of the pandemonium downstairs.

A great deal of the fiendishness of schoolboys and the cruelty of children to their elders is produced just in this way. Elders cannot be superhuman beings and suffering fellow-creatures at the same time. If you pose as a little god, you must pose for better for worse.

HOW LITTLE WE KNOW ABOUT OUR PARENTS

The relation between parent and child has cruel moments for the parent even when money is no object, and the material worries are delegated to servants and school teachers. The child and the parent are strangers to one another necessarily, because their ages must differ widely. Read Goethe's autobiography; and note that though he was happy in his parents and had exceptional powers of observation, divination, and story-telling, he knew less about his father and mother than about most of the other people he mentions. I myself was never on bad terms with my mother: we lived together until I was forty-two years old, absolutely without the smallest friction of any kind, yet when her death set me thinking curiously about our relations, I realized that I knew very little about her. Introduce me to a strange woman who was a child when I was a child, a girl when I was a boy, an adolescent when I was an adolescent; and if we take naturally to one another I will know more of her and she of me at the end of forty days (I had almost said of forty minutes) than I knew of my mother at the end of forty years. A contemporary stranger is a novelty and an enigma, also a possibility; but a mother is like a broomstick or like the sun in the heavens, it does not matter which as far as one's knowledge of her is concerned: the broomstick is there and the sun is there; and whether the child is beaten by it or warmed and enlightened by it, it accepts it as a fact in nature, and does not conceive it as having had youth, passions, and weaknesses, or as still growing, yearning, suffering, and learning. If I meet a widow I may ask her all about her marriage; but what son ever dreams of asking his mother about her marriage, or could endure to hear of it without violently breaking off the old sacred relationship between them, and ceasing to be her child or anything more to her than the first man in the street might be?

Yet though in this sense the child cannot realize its parent's humanity, the parent can realize the child's; for the parents with their experience of life have none of the illusions about the child that the child has about the parents; and the consequence is that the child can hurt its parents' feelings much more than its parents can hurt the child's, because the child, even when there has been none of the deliberate hypocrisy by which children are taken advantage of by their elders, cannot conceive the parent as a fellow-creature, whilst the parents know very well that the children are only themselves over again. The child cannot conceive that its blame or contempt or want of interest could possibly hurt its parent, and therefore expresses them all with an indifference which has given rise to the term *enfant terrible* (a tragic term in spite of the jests connected with it); whilst the parent can suffer from such slights and reproaches more from a child than from anyone else, even when the child is not beloved, because the child is so unmistakably sincere in them.

OUR ABANDONED MOTHERS

Take a very common instance of this agonizing incompatibility. A widow brings up her son to manhood. He meets a strange woman, and goes off with and marries her, leaving his mother desolate. It does not occur to him that this is at all hard on her: he does it as a matter of course, and actually expects his mother to receive, on terms of special affection, the woman for whom she has been abandoned. If he shewed any sense of what he was doing, any remorse; if he mingled his tears with hers and asked her not to think too hardly of him because he had obeyed the inevitable destiny of a man to leave his father and mother and cleave to his wife, she could give him her blessing and accept her bereavement with dignity and without reproach. But the man never dreams of such considerations. To him his mother's feeling in the matter, when she betrays it, is unreasonable, ridiculous, and even odious, as shewing a prejudice against his adorable bride.

I have taken the widow as an extreme and obvious case; but there are many husbands and wives who are tired of their consorts, or disappointed in them, or estranged from them by infidelities; and these parents, in losing a son or a daughter through marriage, may be losing everything they care for. No parent's love is as innocent as the love of a child: the exclusion of all conscious sexual feeling from it does not exclude the bitterness, jealousy, and despair at loss which characterize sexual passion: in fact, what is called a pure love may easily be more selfish and jealous than a carnal one. Anyhow, it is plain matter of fact that naïvely selfish people sometimes try with fierce jealously to prevent their children marrying.

FAMILY AFFECTION

Until the family as we know it ceases to exist, nobody will dare to analyse parental affection as distinguished from that general human sympathy which has secured to many an orphan fonder care in a stranger's house than it would have received from its actual parents. Not even Tolstoy, in The Kreutzer Sonata, has said all that we suspect about it. When it persists beyond the period at which it ceases to be necessary to the child's welfare, it is apt to be morbid; and we are probably wrong to inculcate its deliberate cultivation. The natural course is for the parents and children to cast off the specific parental and filial relation when they are no longer necessary to one another. The child does this readily enough to form fresh ties, closer and more fascinating. Parents are not always excluded from such compensations: it happens sometimes that when the children go out at the door the lover comes in at the window. Indeed it happens now oftener than it used to, because people remain much longer in the sexual arena. The cultivated Jewess no longer cuts off her hair at her marriage. The British matron has discarded her cap and her conscientious ugliness; and a bishop's wife at fifty has more of the air of a *femme galante* than an actress had at thirty-five in her grandmother's time. But as people marry later, the facts of age and time still inexorably condemn most parents to comparative solitude when their children marry. This may be a privation and may be a relief: probably in healthy circumstances it is no worse than a salutary change of habit; but even at that it is, for the moment at least, a wrench. For though parents and children sometimes dislike one another, there is an experience of succor and a habit of dependence and expectation formed in infancy which naturally attaches a child to its parent or to its nurse (a foster parent) in a quite peculiar way. A benefit to the child may be a burden to the parent; but people become attached to their burdens sometimes more than the burdens are attached to them; and to "suffer little children" has become an affectionate impulse deep in our nature.

Now there is no such impulse to suffer our sisters and brothers, our aunts and uncles, much less our cousins. If we could choose our relatives, we might, by selecting congenial ones, mitigate the repulsive effect of the obligation to like them and to admit them to our intimacy. But to have a person imposed on us as a brother merely because he happens to have the same parents is unbearable when, as may easily happen, he is the sort of person we should carefully avoid if he were anyone else's brother. All Europe (except Scotland, which has clans instead of families) draws the line at second cousins. Protestantism draws it still closer by making the first cousin a marriageable stranger; and the only reason for not drawing it at sisters and brothers is that the institution of the family compels us to spend our childhood with them, and thus

imposes on us a curious relation in which familiarity
destroys romantic charm, and is yet expected to create
a specially warm affection. Such a relation is dangerously
factitious and unnatural; and the practical moral is that
the less said at home about specific family affection the
better. Children, like grown-up people, get on well enough
together if they are not pushed down one another's
throats; and grown-up relatives will get on together in
proportion to their separation and their care not to presume on their blood relationship. We should let children's
feelings take their natural course without prompting. I
have seen a child scolded and called unfeeling because it
did not occur to it to make a theatrical demonstration of
affectionate delight when its mother returned after an
absence: a typical example of the way in which spurious
family sentiment is stoked up. We are, after all, sociable
animals; and if we are let alone in the matter of our
affections, and well brought up otherwise, we shall not get
on any the worse with particular people because they
happen to be our brothers and sisters and cousins. The
danger lies in assuming that we shall get on any better.

The main point to grasp here is that families are not
kept together at present by family feeling but by human
feeling. The family cultivates sympathy and mutual help
and consolation as any other form of kindly association
cultivates them; but the addition of a dictated compulsory affection as an attribute of near kinship is not
only unnecessary, but positively detrimental; and the alleged tendency of modern social development to break up
the family need alarm nobody. We cannot break up the
facts of kinship nor eradicate its natural emotional consequences. What we can do and ought to do is to set people
free to behave naturally and to change their behavior as
circumstances change. To impose on a citizen of London
the family duties of a Highland cateran in the eighteenth
century is as absurd as to compel him to carry a claymore
and target instead of an umbrella. The civilized man has
no special use for cousins; and he may presently find that

he has no special use for brothers and sisters. The parent seems likely to remain indispensable; but there is no reason why that natural tie should be made the excuse for unnatural aggravations of it, as crushing to the parent as they are oppressive to the child. The mother and father will not always have to shoulder the burthen of maintenance which should fall on the Atlas shoulders of the fatherland and motherland. Pending such reforms and emancipations, a shattering break-up of the paternal home must remain one of normal incidents of marriage. The parent is left lonely and the child is not. Woe to the old if they have no impersonal interests, no convictions, no public causes to advance, no tastes or hobbies! It is well to be a mother but not to be a mother-in-law; and if men were cut off artificially from intellectual and public interests as women are, the father-in-law would be as deplorable a figure in popular tradition as the mother-in-law.

It is not to be wondered at that some people hold that blood relationship should be kept a secret from the persons related, and that the happiest condition in this respect is that of the foundling who, if he ever meets his parents or brothers or sisters, passes them by without knowing them. And for such a view there is this to be said: that our family system does unquestionably take the natural bond between members of the same family, which, like all natural bonds, is not too tight to be borne, and superimposes on it a painful burden of forced, inculated, suggested, and altogether unnecessary affection and responsibility which we should do well to get rid of by making relatives as independent of one another as possible.

THE FATE OF THE FAMILY

The difficulty of inducing people to talk sensibly about the family is the same as that which I pointed out in a previous volume as confusing discussions of marriage. Marriage is not a single invariable institution: it changes from civilization to civilization, from religion to religion, from civil code to civil code, from frontier to frontier. The family is still more variable, because the number of persons constituting a family, unlike the number of persons constituting a marriage, varies from one to twenty: indeed, when a widower with a family marries a widow with a family, and the two produce a third family, even that very high number may be surpassed. And the conditions may vary between opposite extremes: for example, in a London or Paris slum every child adds to the burden of poverty and helps to starve the parents and all the other children, whereas in a settlement of pioneer colonists every child, from the moment it is big enough to lend a hand to the family industry, is an investment in which the only danger is that of temporary over-capitalization. Then there are the variations in family sentiment. Sometimes the family organization is as frankly political as the organization of an army or an industry: fathers being no more expected to be sentimental about their children than colonels about soldiers, or factory owners about their employees, though the mother may be allowed a little tenderness if her character is weak. The Roman father was a despot: the Chinese father is an object of worship: the sentimental modern western father is often a playfellow looked to for toys and pocket-money. The farmers sees his children constantly: the squire sees them only during the holidays, and not then oftener than he can help: the tram conductor, when employed by a joint stock company, sometimes never sees them at all.

Under such circumstances phrases like The Influence of Home Life, The Family, The Domestic Hearth, and so on, are no more specific than The Mammals, or The Man In The Street; and the pious generalizations founded so glibly on them by our sentimental moralists are unworkable. When households average twelve persons with the sexes about equally represented, the results may be fairly good. When they average three the results may be very bad indeed; and to lump the two together under the general term The Family is to confuse the question hopelessly. The modern small family is much too stuffy: children "brought up at home" in it are unfit for society.

But here again circumstances differ. If the parents live in what is called a garden suburb, where there is a good deal of social intercourse, and the family, instead of keeping itself to itself, as the evil old saying is, and glowering at the neighbors over the blinds of the long street in which nobody knows his neighbor and everyone wishes to deceive him as to his income and social importance, is in effect broken up by school life, by out-of-door habits, and by frank neighborly intercourse through dances and concerts and theatricals and excursions and the like, families of four may turn out much less barbarous citizens than families of ten which attain the Boer ideal of being out of sight of one another's chimney smoke.

All one can say is, roughly, that the homelier the home, and the more familiar the family, the worse for everybody concerned. The family ideal is a humbug and a nuisance: one might as reasonably talk of the barrack ideal, or the forecastle ideal, or any other substitution of the machinery of social organization for the end of it, which must always be the fullest and most capable life: in short, the most godly life. And this significant word reminds us that though the popular conception of heaven includes a Holy Family, it does not attach to that family the notion of a separate home, or a private nursery or kitchen or mother-in-law, or anything that constitutes the family as we know it. Even blood relationship is miraculously abstracted from it; and the Father is the father of all children, the mother the mother of all mothers and babies, and the Son the Son of Man and the Savior of his brothers: one whose chief utterance on the subject of the conventional family was an invitation to all of us to leave our families and follow him, and to leave the dead to bury the dead, and not debauch ourselves at that gloomy festival the family funeral, with its sequel of hideous mourning and grief which is either affected or morbid.

FAMILY MOURNING

I do not know how far this detestable custom of mourning is carried in France; but judging from the appearance of the French people I should say that a Frenchwoman goes into mourning for her cousins to the seventeenth degree. The result is that when I cross the Channel I seem to have reached a country devastated by war or pestilence. It is really suffering only from the family. Will anyone pretend that England has not the better of this striking difference? It is such senseless and unnatural conventions as this that make us so impatient of what we call family feeling. Even apart from its insufferable pretensions, the family needs hearty discrediting; for there is hardly any vulnerable part of it that could not be amputated with advantage.

ART TEACHING

By art teaching I hasten to say that I do not mean giving children lessons in freehand drawing and perspective. I am simply calling attention to the fact that fine art is the only teacher except torture. I have already pointed out that nobody, except under threat of torture, can read a school book. The reason is that a school book is not a work of art. Similarly, you cannot listen to a lesson or a sermon unless the teacher or the preacher is an artist. You cannot read the Bible if you have no sense of literary art. The reason why the continental European is, to the Englishman or American, so surprisingly ignorant of the Bible, is that the authorized English version is a great work of literary art, and the continental versions are comparatively artless. To read a dull book; to listen to a tedious play or prosy sermon or lecture; to stare at uninteresting pictures or ugly buildings: nothing, short of disease, is more dreadful than this. The violence done to our souls by it leaves injuries and produces subtle maladies which have never been properly studied by psychopathologists. Yet we are so inured to it in school, where practically all the teachers are bores trying to do the work of artists, and all the books artless, that we acquire a truly frightful power of enduring boredom. We even acquire the notion that fine art is lascivious and destructive to the character. In Church, in the House of Commons, at public meetings, we sit solemnly listening to bores and twaddlers because from the time we could walk or speak we have been snubbed, scolded, bullied, beaten and imprisoned whenever we dared to resent being bored or twaddled at, or to express our natural impatience and derision of bores and twaddlers. And when a man arises with a soul of sufficient native strength to break the bonds of this inculcated reverence and to expose and deride and tweak the noses of our humbugs and panjandrums, like Voltaire or Dickens, we are shocked and scandalized, even when we cannot help laughing. Worse, we dread and persecute those who can see and declare the truth, because their sincerity and insight reflects on our delusion and blindness. We are all like Nell Gwynne's footman, who defended Nell's reputation with his fists, not because he believed her to be what he called an honest woman, but because he objected to be scorned as the footman of one who was no better than she should be.

This wretched power of allowing ourselves to be bored may seem to give the fine arts a chance sometimes. People will sit through a performance of Beethoven's ninth symphony or of Wagner's Ring just as they will sit through a dull sermon or a front bench politician saying nothing for two hours whilst his unfortunate country is perishing through the delay of its business in Parliament. But their endurance is very bad for the ninth symphony, because they never hiss when it is murdered. I have heard an Italian conductor (no longer living) take the *adagio* of that symphony at a lively *allegretto*, slowing down for the warmer major sections into the speed and manner of the heroine's death song in a Verdi opera; and the listeners, far from relieving my excrucation by rising with yells of fury and hurling their programs and opera glasses at the miscreant, behaved just as they do when Richter conducts it. The mass of imposture that thrives on this combination of ignorance with despairing endurance is incalculable. Given a public trained from childhood to stand anything tedious, and so saturated with school discipline that even with the doors open and no schoolmasters to stop them they will sit there helplessly until the end of the concert or opera gives them leave to go home; and you will have in great capitals hundreds of thousands of pounds spent every night in the season on professedly artistic entertainments which have no other effect on fine art than to exacerbate the hatred in which it is already secretly held in England.

Fortunately, there are arts that cannot be cut off from the people by bad performances. We can read books for ourselves; and we can play a good deal of fine music for ourselves with the help of a pianola. Nothing stands between us and the actual handwork of the great masters of painting except distance; and modern photographic methods of reproduction are in some cases quite and in many nearly as effective in conveying the artist's message as a modern edition of Shakespear's plays is in conveying the message that first existed in his handwriting. The reproduction of great feats of musical execution is already on the way: the gramophone, for all its wheezing and snarling and braying, is steadily improving in its manners; and what with this improvement on the one hand, and on the other that blessed selective faculty which enables us to ignore a good deal of disagreeable noise if there is a thread of music in the middle of it (few critics of the gramophone seem to be conscious of the very considerable mechanical noise set up by choirs and orchestras) we have at last reached a point at which, for example, a person living in an English village where the church music is the only music, and that music is made by a few well-intentioned ladies with the help of a harmonium, can hear masses by Palestrina very passably executed, and can thereby be led to the discovery that Jackson in F and Hymns Ancient and Modern are not perhaps the last word of beauty and propriety in the praise of God.

In short, there is a vast body of art now within the reach of everybody. The difficulty is that this art, which alone can educate us in grace of body and soul, and which alone can make the history of the past live for us or the hope of the future shine for us, which alone can give delicacy and nobility to our crude lusts, which is the appointed vehicle of inspiration and the method of the communion of saints, is actually branded as sinful among us because, wherever it arises, there is resistance to tyranny, breaking of fetters, and the breath of freedom. The attempt to suppress art is not wholly successful: we might as well try to suppress oxygen. But it is carried far enough to inflict on huge numbers of people a most injurious art starvation, and to corrupt a great deal of the art that is tolerated. You will find in England plenty of rich families with little more culture than their dogs and horses. And you will find poor families, cut off by poverty and town life from the contemplation of the beauty of the earth, with its dresses of leaves, its scarves of cloud, and its contours of hill and valley, who would positively be happier as hogs, so little have they cultivated their humanity by the only effective instrument of culture: art. The dearth is artificially maintained even when there are the means of satisfying it. Story books are forbidden, picture post cards are forbidden, theatres are forbidden, operas are forbidden, circuses are forbidden, sweetmeats are forbidden, pretty colors are forbidden, all exactly as vice is forbidden. The Creator is explicitly prayed to, and implicitly convicted of indecency every day. An association of vice and sin with everything that is delightful and of goodness with everything that is wretched and detestable is set up. All the most perilous (and glorious) appetites and propensities are at once inflamed by starvation and uneducated by art. All the wholesome conditions which art imposes on appetite are waived: instead of cultivated men and women restrained by a thousand delicacies, repelled by ugliness, chilled by vulgarity, horrified by coarseness, deeply and sweetly moved by the graces that art has revealed to them and nursed in them, we get indiscriminate rapacity in pursuit of pleasure and a parade of the grossest stimulations in catering for it. We have a continual clamor for goodness, beauty, virtue, and sanctity, with such an appalling inability to recognize it or love it when it arrives that it is more dangerous to be a great prophet or poet than to promote twenty companies for swindling simple folk out of their savings. Do not for a moment suppose that uncultivated people are merely indifferent to high and noble qualities. They hate them malignantly. At best, such qualities are like rare and beautiful birds: when they appear the whole country takes down its guns; but the birds receive the statuary tribute of having their corpses stuffed.

And it really all comes from the habit of preventing children from being troublesome. You are so careful of your boy's morals, knowing how troublesome they may be, that you keep him away from the Venus of Milo only to find him in the arms of the scullery maid or someone much worse. You decide that the Hermes of Praxiteles and Wagner's Tristan are not suited for young girls; and your daughter marries somebody appallingly unlike either Hermes or Tristan solely to escape from your parental protection. You have not stifled a single passion nor averted a single danger: you have depraved the passions by starving them, and broken down all the defences which so effectively protect children brought up in freedom. You have men who imagine themselves to be ministers of religion openly declaring that when they pass through the streets they have to keep out in the wheeled traffic to avoid the temptations of the pavement. You have them organizing hunts of the women who tempt them—poor creatures whom no artist would touch without a shudder— and wildly clamoring for more clothes to disguise and conceal the body, and for the abolition of pictures, statues, theatres, and pretty colors. And incredible as it seems, these unhappy lunatics are left at large, unrebuked, even admired and revered, whilst artists have to struggle for toleration. To them an undraped human body is the most monstrous, the most blighting, the most obscene, the most unbearable spectacle in the universe. To an artist it is, at its best, the most admirable spectacle in nature, and, at its average, an object of indifference. If every rag of clothing miraculously dropped from the inhabitants of London at noon tomorrow (say as a preliminary to the Great Judgment), the artistic people would not turn a hair; but the artless people would go mad and call on the mountains to hide them. I submit that this indicates a thoroughly healthy state on the part of the artists, and a thoroughly morbid one on the part of the artless. And the healthy state is attainable in a cold country like ours only by familiarity with the undraped figure acquired through pictures, statues, and theatrical representations in which an illusion of natural clotheslessness is produced and made poetic.

In short, we all grow up stupid and mad to just the extent to which we have not been artistically educated; and the fact that this taint of stupidity and madness has to be tolerated because it is general, and is even boasted of as characteristically English, makes the situation all the worse. It is becoming exceedingly grave at present, because the last ray of art is being cut off from our schools by the discontinuance of religious education.

THE IMPOSSIBILITY OF SECULAR EDUCATION

Now children must be taught some sort of religion. Secular education is an impossibility. Secular education comes to this: that the only reason for ceasing to do evil and learning to do well is that if you do not you will be caned. This is worse than being taught in a church school that if you become a dissenter you will go to hell; for hell is presented as the instrument of something eternal, divine, and inevitable: you cannot evade it at the moment the school-master's back is turned. What confuses this issue and leads even highly intelligent religious persons to advocate secular education as a means of rescuing children from the strife of rival proselytizers is the failure to distinguish between the child's personal subjective need for a religion and its right to an impartially communicated historical objective knowledge of all the creeds and Churches. Just as a child, no matter what its race and color may be, should know that there are black men and brown men and yellow men, and, no matter what its political convictions may be, that there are Monarchists and Republicans and Positivists, Socialists and Unsocialists, so it should know that there are Christians and Mahometans and Buddhists and Shintoists and so forth, and that they are on the average just as honest and well-behaved as its own father. For example, it should not be told that Allah is a false god set up by the Turks and Arabs, who will all be damned for taking that liberty; but it should be told that many English people think so, and that many Turks and Arabs think the converse about English people. It should be taught that Allah is simply the name by which God is known to Turks and Arabs, who are just as eligible for salvation as any Christian. Further, that the practical reason why a Turkish child should pray in a mosque and an English child in a church is that as worship is organized in Turkey in mosques in the name of Mahomet and in England in churches in the name of Christ, a Turkish child joining the Church of England or an English child following Mahomet will find that it has no place for its worship and no organization of its religion within its reach. Any other teaching of the history and present facts of religion is false teaching, and is politically extremely dangerous in an empire in which a huge majority of the fellow-subjects of the governing island do not profess the religion of that island.

But this objectivity, though intellectually honest, tells

the child only what other people believe. What it should itself believe is quite another matter. The sort of Rationalism which says to a child "You must suspend your judgment until you are old enough to choose your religion" is Rationalism gone mad. The child must have a conscience and a code of honor (which is the essence of religion) even if it be only a provisional one, to be revised at its confirmation. For confirmation is meant to signalize a spiritual coming of age, and may be a repudiation. Really active souls have many confirmations and repudiations as their life deepens and their knowledge widens. But what is to guide the child before its first confirmation? Not mere orders, because orders must have a sanction of some sort or why should the child obey them? If, as a Secularist, you refuse to teach any sanction, you must say "You will be punished if you disobey." "Yes," says the child to itself, "if I am found out; but wait until your back is turned and I will do as I like, and lie about it." There can be no objective punishment for successful fraud; and as no espionage can cover the whole range of a child's conduct, the upshot is that the child becomes a liar and schemer with an atrophied conscience. And a good many of the orders given to it are not obeyed after all. Thus the Secularist who is not a fool is forced to appeal to the child's vital impulse towards perfection, to the divine spark; and no resolution not to call this impulse an impulse of loyalty to the Fellowship of the Holy Ghost, or obedience to the Will of God, or any other standard theological term, can alter the fact that the Secularist has stepped outside Secularism and is educating the child religiously, even if he insists on repudiating that pious adverb and substituting the word metaphysically.

NATURAL SELECTION AS A RELIGION

We must make up our minds to it therefore that whatever measures we may be forced to take to prevent the recruiting sergeants of the Churches, free or established, from ob-

taining an exclusive right of entry to schools, we shall
not be able to exclude religion from them. The most horrible of all religions: that which teaches us to regard ourselves as the helpless prey of a series of senseless accidents
called Natural Selection, is allowed and even welcomed
in so-called secular schools because it is, in a sense, the
negation of all religion; but for school purposes a religion
is a belief which affects conduct: and no belief affects
conduct more radically and often so disastrously as the
belief that the universe is a product of Natural Selection.
What is more, the theory of Natural Selection cannot
be kept out of schools, because many of the natural facts
that present the most plausible appearance of design can
be accounted for by Natural Selection; and it would be
as absurd to keep a child in delusive ignorance of so
potent a factor in evolution as to keep it in ignorance
of radiation or capillary attraction. Even if you make a
religion of Natural Selection, and teach the child to regard
itself as the irresponsible prey of its circumstances and
appetites (or its heredity as you will perhaps call them),
you will none the less find that its appetites are stimulated
by your encouragement and daunted by your discourage-
ment; that one of its appetites is an appetite for perfection; that if you discourage this appetite and encourage
the cruder acquisitive appetites the child will steal and
lie and be a nuisance to you; and that if you encourage
its appetite for perfection and teach it to attach a peculiar
sacredness to it and place it before the other appetites, it
will be a much nicer child and you will have a much easier
job, at which point you will, in spite of your pseudo-
scientific jargon, find yourself back in the old-fashioned
religious teaching as deep as Dr Watts and in fact fathoms
deeper.

MORAL INSTRUCTION LEAGUES

And now the voices of our Moral Instruction Leagues
will be lifted, asking whether there is any reason why

the appetite for perfection should not be cultivated in
rationally scientific terms instead of being associated with
the story of Jonah and the great fish and the thousand
other tales that grow up round religions. Yes: there are
many reasons; and one of them is that children all like
the story of Jonah and the whale (they insist on its being
a whale in spite of demonstrations by Bible smashers
without any sense of humor that Jonah would not have
fitted into a whale's gullet—as if the story would be credible of a whale with an enlarged throat) and that no child
on earth can stand moral instruction books or catechisms
or any other statement of the case for religion in abstract
terms. The object of a moral instruction book is not to be
rational, scientific, exact, proof against controversy, nor
even credible: its object is to make children good. If it
makes them sick instead its place is the waste-paper
basket. And if it is to be read it must be readable.

Take for an illustration the story of Elisha and the
bears. To the authors of the moral instruction books it is
in the last degree reprehensible. It is obviously not true
as a record of fact; and the picture it gives us of the
temper of God (which is what interests an adult reader)
is shocking and blasphemous. But it is a capital story for
a child. It interests a child because it is about bears; and
it leaves the child with an impression that children who
poke fun at old gentlemen and make rude remarks about
bald heads are not nice children, which is a highly desirable impression, and just as much as a child is capable of
receiving from the story. When a story is about God and a
child, children take God for granted and criticize the child.
Adults do the opposite, and are thereby often led to talk
great nonsense about the bad effect of Bible stories on
infants.

But let no one think that a child or anyone else can
learn religion from a teacher or a book or by any academic
process whatever. It is only by an unfettered access to the
whole body of Fine Art: that is, to the whole body of
inspired revelation, that we can build up that conception

of divinity to which all virtue is an aspiration. And to hope to find this body of art purified from all that is obsolete or dangerous or fierce or lusty, or to pick and choose what will be good for any particular child, much less for all children, is the shallowest of vanities. Such schoolmasterly selection is neither possible nor desirable. Ignorance of evil is not virtue but imbecility: admiring it is like giving a prize for honesty to a man who has not stolen your watch because he did not know you had one. Virtue chooses good from evil; and without knowledge there can be no choice. And even this is a dangerous simplification of what actually occurs. We are not choosing: we are growing. Were you to cut all of what you call the evil out of a child, it would drop dead. If you try to stretch it to full human stature when it is ten years old, you will simply pull it into two pieces and be hanged. And when you try to do this morally, which is what parents and schoolmasters are doing every day, you ought to be hanged; and some day, when we take a sensible view of the matter, you will be; and serve you right. The child does not stand between a good and a bad angel: what it has to deal with is a middling angel who, in normal healthy cases, wants to be a good angel as fast as it can without killing itself in the process, which is a dangerous one.

Therefore there is no question of providing the child with a carefully regulated access to good art. There is no good art, any more than there is good anything else in the absolute sense. Art that is too good for the child will either teach it nothing or drive it mad, as the Bible has driven many people mad who might have kept their sanity had they been allowed to read much lower forms of literature. The practical moral is that we must read whatever stories, see whatever pictures, hear whatever songs and symphonies, go to whatever plays we like. We shall not like those which have nothing to say to us; and though everyone has a right to bias our choice, no one has a right to deprive us of it by keeping us from any work of art or any work of art from us.

I may now say without danger of being misunderstood that the popular English compromise called Cowper-Templeism (unsectarian Bible education) is not so silly as it looks. It is true that the Bible inculcates half a dozen religions: some of them barbarous; some cynical and pessimistic; some amoristic and romantic; some sceptical and challenging; some kindly, simple, and intuitional; some sophistical and intellectual; none suited to the character and conditions of western civilization unless it be the Christianity which was finally suppressed by the Crucifixion, and has never been put into practice by any State before or since. But the Bible contains the ancient literature of a very remarkable Oriental race; and the imposition of this literature, on whatever false pretences, on our children left them more literate than if they knew no literature at all, which was the practical alternative. And as our Authorized Version is a great work of art as well, to know it was better than knowing no art, which also was the practical alternative. It is at least not a school book; and it is not a bad story book, horrible as some of the stories are. Therefore as between the Bible and the blank represented by secular education in its most matter-of-fact sense, the choice is with the Bible.

THE BIBLE

But the Bible is not sufficient. The real Bible of modern Europe is the whole body of great literature in which the inspiration and revelation of Hebrew Scripture has been continued to the present day. Nietzsche's Thus Spake Zoroaster is less comforting to the ill and unhappy than the Psalms; but it is much truer, subtler, and more edifying. The pleasure we get from the rhetoric of the book of Job and its tragic picture of a bewildered soul cannot disguise the ignoble irrelevance of the retort of God with which it closes, nor supply the need for such modern revelations as Shelley's Prometheus or The Niblung's Ring of Richard Wagner. There is nothing in the Bible greater in inspiration than Beethoven's ninth symphony; and the power of modern music to convey that inspiration to a modern man is far greater than that of Elizabethan English, which is, except for people steeped in the Bible from childhood like Sir Walter Scott and Ruskin, a dead language.

Besides, many who have no ear for literature or for music are accessible to architecture, to pictures, to statues, to dresses, and to the arts of the stage. Every device of art should be brought to bear on the young; so that they may discover some form of it that delights them naturally; for there will come to all of them that period between dawning adolescence and full maturity when the pleasures and emotions of art will have to satisfy cravings which, it starved or insulted, may become morbid and seek disgraceful satisfactions, and, if prematurely gratified otherwise than poetically, may destroy the stamina of the race. And it must be borne in mind that the most dangerous art for this necessary purpose is the art that presents itself as religious ecstasy. Young people are ripe for love long before they are ripe for religion. Only a very foolish person would substitute the Imitation of Christ for Treasure Island as a present for a boy or girl, or for Byron's Don Juan as a present for a swain or lass. Pickwick is the safest saint for us in our nonage. Flaubert's Temptation of St Anthony is an excellent book for a man of fifty, perhaps the best within reach as a healthy study of visionary ecstasy; but for the purposes of a boy of fifteen Ivanhoe and the Templar make a much better saint and devil. And the boy of fifteen will find this out for himself if he is allowed to wander in a well-stocked literary garden, and hear bands and see pictures and spend his pennies on cinematograph shows. His choice may often be rather disgusting to his elders when they want him to choose the best before he is ready for it. The greatest Protestant Manifesto ever written, as far as I know, is Houston

Chamberlain's Foundations of the Nineteenth Century: everybody capable of it should read it. Probably the History of Maria Monk is at the opposite extreme of merit (this is a guess: I have never read it); but it is certain that a boy let loose in a library would go for Maria Monk and have no use whatever for Mr Chamberlain. I should probably have read Maria Monk myself if I had not had the Arabian Nights and their like to occupy me better. In art, children, like adults, will find their level if they are left free to find it, and not restricted to what adults think good for them. Just at present our young people are going mad over ragtimes, apparently because syncopated rhythms are new to them. If they had learnt what can be done with syncopation from Beethoven's third Leonora overture, they would enjoy the ragtimes all the more; but they would put them in their proper place as amusing vulgarities.

ARTIST IDOLATRY

But there are more dangerous influences than ragtimes waiting for people brought up in ignorance of fine art. Nothing is more pitiably ridiculous than the wild worship of artists by those who have never been seasoned in youth to the enchantments of art. Tenors and prima donnas, pianists and violinists, actors and actresses enjoy powers of seduction which in the middle ages would have exposed them to the risk of being burnt for sorcery. But as they exercise this power by singing, playing, and acting, no great harm is done except perhaps to themselves. Far graver are the powers enjoyed by brilliant persons who are also connoisseurs in art. The influence they can exercise on young people who have been brought up in the darkness and wretchedness of a home without art, and in whom a natural bent towards art has always been baffled and snubbed, is incredible to those who have not witnessed and understood it. He (or she) who reveals the world of art to them opens heaven to them. They become satellites, disciples, worshippers of the apostle. Now the apostle may be a voluptuary without much conscience. Nature may have given him enough virtue to suffice in a reasonable environment. But this allowance may not be enough to defend him against the temptation and demoralization of finding himself a little god on the strength of what ought to be a quite ordinary culture. He may find adorers in all directions in our uncultivated society among people of stronger character than himself, not one of whom, if they had been artistically educated, would have had anything to learn from him or regarded him as in any way extraordinary apart from his actual achievements as an artist. Tartuffe is not always a priest. Indeed he is not always a rascal: he is often a weak man absurdly credited with omniscience and perfection, and taking unfair advantages only because they are offered to him and he is too weak to refuse. Give everyone his culture, and no one will offer him more than his due.

In thus delivering our children from the idolatry of the artist, we shall not destroy for them the enchantment of art: on the contrary, we shall teach them to demand art everywhere as a condition attainable by cultivating the body, mind, and heart. Art, said Morris, is the expression of pleasure in work. And certainly, when work is made detestable by slavery, there is no art. It is only when learning is made a slavery by tyrannical teachers that art becomes loathsome to the pupil.

"THE MACHINE"

When we set to work at a Constitution to secure freedom for children, we had better bear in mind that the children may not be at all obliged to us for our pains. Rousseau said that men are born free; and this dangerous saying, as Rousseau meant it, was and is a great and true saying; yet let it not lead us into the error of supposing that all men long for freedom and embrace it when it is offered to them. On the contrary, it has to be forced on them; and even then they will give it the slip if it is not religiously inculcated and strongly safe-guarded.

Besides, men are born docile, and must in the nature of things remain so with regard to everything they do not understand. Now political science and the art of government are among the things they do not understand, and indeed are not at present allowed to understand. They can be enslaved by a system, as we are at present, because it happens to be there, and nobody understands it. An intelligently worked Capitalist system, as Comte saw, would give us all that most of us are intelligent enough to want. What makes it produce such unspeakably vile results is that it is an automatic system which is as little understood by those who profit by it in money as by those who are starved and degraded by it: our millionaires and statesmen are manifestly no more "captains of industry" or scientific politicians than our bookmakers are mathematicians. For some time past a significant word has been coming into use as a substitute for Destiny, Fate, and Providence. It is "The Machine": the machine that has no god in it. Why do governments do nothing in spite of reports of Royal Commissions that establish the most frightful urgency? Why do our philanthropic millionaires do nothing, though they are ready to throw bucketfuls of gold into the streets? The Machine will not let them. Always The Machine. In short, they dont know how. They try to reform Society as an old lady might try to restore a broken down locomotive by prodding it with a knitting needle. And this is not at all because they are born fools, but because they have been educated, not into manhood and freedom, but into blindness and slavery by their parents and schoolmasters, themselves the victims of a similar misdirection, and consequently of The Machine. They do not want liberty. They have not been educated to want it. They choose slavery and inequality; and all the other evils are automatically added to them.

And yet we must have The Machine. It is only in unskilled hands under ignorant direction that machinery is dangerous. We can no more govern modern communities without political machinery than we can feed and clothe them without industrial machinery. Shatter The Machine, and you get Anarchy. And yet The Machine works so destestably at present that we have people who advocate anarchy and call themselves Anarchists.

THE PROVOCATION TO ANARCHISM

The Anarchists are right when they say that Governments, like schoolmasters, try to simplify their task by destroying liberty and glorifying authority, especially their own. But the difficulty of combining law and order with free institutions is not a natural one. It is a matter of inculcation. If people are brought up to be slaves, it is useless and dangerous to let them loose at the age of twenty-one and say "Now you are free." No one with the tamed soul and broken spirit of a slave can be free. It is like saying to a laborer brought up on a family income of thirteen shillings a week, "Here is one hundred thousand pounds: now you are wealthy." Nothing can make such a man really wealthy. Freedom and wealth are difficult and responsible conditions to which men must be accustomed and socially trained from birth. A nation that is free at twenty-one is not free at all; just as a man first enriched at fifty remains poor all his life, even if he does not curtail it by drinking himself to death in the first wild ecstasy of being able to swallow as much as he likes for the first time. You cannot govern men brought up as slaves otherwise than as slaves are governed. You may pile Bills of Right and Habeas Corpus Acts on Great Charters; promulgate American Constitutions; burn the chateaux and guillotine the seigneurs; chop off the heads of kings and queens and set up Democracy on the ruins of feudalism: the end of it all for us is that already in the twentieth century there has been as much brute coercion and savage intolerance, as much flogging and hanging, as much impudent injustice on the bench and lustful rancor in the pulpit, as much naïve resort to torture, persecution, and suppression of free speech and freedom of the press, as much war, as much of the vilest excess of mutilation, rapine, and delirious indiscriminate slaughter of helpless non-combatants, old and young, as much prostitution of professional talent, literary and political, in defence of manifest wrong, as much cowardly sycophancy giving fine names to all this villainy or pretending that it is "greatly exaggerated," as we can find any record of from the days when the advocacy of liberty was a capital offence and Democracy was hardly thinkable. Democracy exhibits the vanity of Louis XIV, the savagery of Peter of Russia, the nepotism and provinciality of Napoleon, the fickleness of Catherine II: in short, all the childishnesses of all the despots without any of the qualities that enabled the greatest of them to fascinate and dominate their contemporaries.

And the flatterers of Democracy are as impudently servile to the successful, and insolent to common honest folk, as the flatterers of the monarchs. Democracy in America has led to the withdrawal of ordinary refined persons from politics; and the same result is coming in England as fast as we make Democracy as democratic as it is in America. This is true also of popular religion: it is so horribly irreligious that nobody with the smallest pretence to culture, or the least inkling of what the great prophets vainly tried to make the world understand, will have anything to do with it except for purely secular reasons.

IMAGINATION

Before we can clearly understand how baleful is this condition of intimidation in which we live, it is necessary to clear up the confusion made by our use of the word imagination to denote two very different powers of mind. One is the power to imagine things as they are not: this I call the romantic imagination. The other is the power to imagine things as they are without actually sensing them; and this I will call the realistic imagination. Take for example marriage and war. One man has a vision of perpetual bliss with a domestic angel at home, and of flashing sabres, thundering guns, victorious cavalry charges, and routed enemies in the field. That is romantic imagination; and the mischief it does is incalculable. It begins in silly and selfish expectations of the impossible, and ends in spiteful disappointment, sour grievance, cynicism, and misanthropic resistance to any attempt to better a hopeless world. The wise man knows that imagination is not only a means of pleasing himself and beguiling tedious hours with romances and fairy tales and fools' paradises (a quite defensible and delightful amusement when you know exactly what you are doing and where fancy ends and facts begin), but also a means of foreseeing and being prepared for realities as yet unexperienced, and of testing the feasibility and desirability of serious Utopias. He does not expect his wife to be angel; nor does he overlook the facts that war depends on the rousing of all the murderous blackguardism still latent in mankind; that every victory means a defeat; that fatigue, hunger, terror, and disease are the raw material which romancers work up into military glory; and that soldiers for the most part go to war as children go to school, because they are afraid not to. They are afraid even to say they are afraid, as such candor is punishable by death in the military code.

A very little realistic imagination gives an ambitious person enormous power over the multitudinous victims of the romantic imagination. For the romancer not only pleases himself with fictitious glories: he also terrifies himself with imaginary dangers. He does not even picture what these dangers are: he conceives the unknown as always dangerous. When you say to a realist "You must do this" or "You must not do that," he instantly asks what will happen to him if he does (or does not, as the case may be). Failing an unromantic convincing answer, he does just as he pleases unless he can find for himself a real reason for refraining. In short, though you can intimidate him, you cannot bluff him. But you can always bluff the romantic person: indeed his grasp of real considerations is so feeble that you find it necessary to bluff him even when you have solid considerations to offer him instead. The campaigns of Napoleon, with their atmosphere of glory, illustrate this. In the Russian campaign Napoleon's marshals achieved miracles of bluff, especially Ney, who, with a handful of men, monstrously outnumbered, repeatedly kept the Russian troups paralysed with terror by pure bounce. Napoleon himself, much more a realist than Ney (that was why he dominated him), would probably have surrendered; for sometimes the bravest of the brave will achieve successes never attempted by the cleverest of clever. Wellington was a completer realist than Napoleon. It was impossible to persuade Wellington that he was beaten until he actually was beaten. He was unbluffable; and if Napoleon had understood the nature of Wellington's strength instead of returning Wellington's snobbish contempt for him by an academic contempt for Wellington, he would not have left the attack at Waterloo to Ney and D'Erlon, who, on that field, did not know when they were beaten, whereas Wellington knew precisely when he was not beaten. The unbluffable would have triumphed anyhow, probably, because Napoleon was an academic soldier, doing the academic thing (the attack in columns and so forth) with superlative ability and energy; whilst Wellington was an original soldier who, instead of outdoing the terrible academic columns with still more terrible and academic columns, outwitted them with the thin red line, not of heroes, but, as this uncompromising realist never hesitated to testify, of the scum of the earth.

GOVERNMENT BY BULLIES

These picturesque martial incidents are being reproduced every day in our ordinary life. We are bluffed by hardy simpletons and headstrong bounders as the Russians were bluffed by Ney; and our Wellingtons are threadbound by slave-democracy as Gulliver was threadbound by the Lilliputians. We are a mass of people living in a submissive routine to which we have been drilled from our childhood. When you ask us to take the simplest step outside that routine, we say shyly, "Oh, I really couldnt," or "Oh, I shouldnt like to," without being able to point out the smallest harm that could possibly ensue: victims, not of a rational fear of real dangers, but of pure abstract fear, the quintessence of cowardice, the very negation of "the fear of God." Dotted about among us are a few spirits relatively free from this inculcated paralysis, sometimes because they are half-witted, sometimes because they are unscrupulously selfish, sometimes because they are realists as to money and unimaginative as to other things, sometimes even because they are exceptionally able, but always because they are not afraid of shadows nor oppressed with nightmares. And we see these few rising as if by magic into power and affluence, and forming, with the millionaires who have accidentally gained huge riches by the occasional windfalls of our commerce, the governing class. Now nothing is more disastrous than a governing class that does not know how to govern. And how can this rabble of the casual products of luck, cunning, and folly, be expected to know how to govern? The merely lucky ones and the hereditary ones do not owe their position to their qualifications at all. As to the rest, the realism which seems their essential qualification often consists not only in a lack of romantic imagination, which lack is a merit, but of the realistic, constructive, Utopian imagination, which lack is a ghastly defect. Freedom from imaginative illusion is therefore no guarantee whatever of nobility of character: that is why inculcated submissiveness makes us slaves to people much worse than ourselves, and why it is so important that submissiveness should no longer be inculcated.

And yet as long as you have the compulsory school

as we know it, we shall have submissiveness inculcated. What is more, until the active hours of child life are organized separately from the active hours of adults life, so that adults can enjoy the society of children in reason without being tormented, disturbed, harried, burdened, and hindered in their work by them as they would be now if there were no compulsory schools and no children hypnotized into the belief that they must tamely go to them and be imprisoned and beaten and over-tasked in them, we shall have schools under one pretext or another; and we shall have all the evil consequences and all the social hopelessness that result from turning a nation of potential freemen and freewomen into a nation of two-legged spoilt spaniels with everything crushed out of their nature except dread of the whip. Liberty is the breath of life to nations; and liberty is the one thing that parents, schoolmasters, and rulers spend their lives in extirpating for the sake of an immediately quiet and finally disastrous life.

JOHNNY TARLETON, *an ordinary young business man of thirty or less, is taking his weekly Friday to Tuesday in the house of his father,* JOHN TARLETON, *who has made a great deal of money out of Tarleton's Underwear. The house is in Surrey, on the slope of Hindhead; and* JOHNNY, *reclining, novel in hand, in a swinging chair with a little awning above it, is enshrined in a spacious half hemisphere of glass which forms a pavilion commanding the garden, and, beyond it, a barren but lovely landscape of hill profile with fir trees, commons of bracken and gorse, and wonderful cloud pictures.*

The glass pavilion springs from a bridgelike arch in the wall of the house, through which one comes into a big hall with tiled flooring, which suggests that the proprietor's notion of domestic luxury is founded on the lounges of week-end hotels. The arch is not quite in the centre of the wall. There is more wall to JOHNNY'S right than to his left; and this space is occupied by a hat rack and umbrella stand in which tennis rackets, white parasols, caps, Panama hats, and other summery articles are bestowed. Just through the arch at this corner stands a new portable Turkish bath, recently unpacked, with its crate beside it, and on the crate the drawn nails and the hammer used in unpacking. Near the crate are open boxes of garden games: bowls and croquet. Nearly in the middle of the glass wall of the pavilion is a door giving on the garden, with a couple of steps to surmount the hot-water pipes which skirt the glass. At intervals round the pavilion are marble pillars with specimens of Viennese pottery on them, very flamboyant in color and florid in design. Between them are folded garden chairs flung anyhow against the pipes. In the side walls are two doors: one near the hat stand, leading to the interior of the house, the

119

*other on the opposite side and at the other end, lead-
ing to the vestibule.*

*There is no solid furniture except a sideboard which
stands against the wall between the vestibule door
and the pavilion, a small writing table with blotter,
rack for telegram forms and stationery, and a waste-
paper basket, standing out in the hall near the sideboard, and a lady's worktable, with two chairs at it,
towards the other side of the lounge. The writing
table has also two chairs at it. On the sideboard there
is a tantalus, liqueur bottles, a syphon, a glass jug
of lemonade, tumblers, and every convenience for
casual drinking. Also a plate of sponge-cakes, and a
highly ornate punchbowl in the same style as the
keramic display in the pavilion. Wicker chairs and
little bamboo tables with ash trays and boxes of
matches on them are scattered in all directions. In
the pavilion, which is flooded with sunshine, is the
elaborate patent swing seat and awning in which
JOHNNY reclines with his novel. There are two wicker
chairs right and left of him.*

BENTLEY SUMMERHAYS, *one of those smallish, thin-
skinned youths, who from 17 to 70 retain unaltered
the mental airs of the later and the physical appearance of the earlier age, appears in the garden and
comes through the glass door into the pavilion. He
is unmistakably a grade above* JOHNNY *socially; and
though he looks sensitive enough, his assurance and
his high voice are a little exasperating.*

JOHNNY. Hallo! Wheres your luggage?

BENTLEY. I left it at the station. Ive walked up from
Haslemere. (*He goes to the hat stand and hangs up his
hat*).

JOHNNY. (*shortly*) Oh! And whos to fetch it?

BENTLEY. Dont know. Dont care. Providence, probably. If not, your mother will have it fetched.

JOHNNY. Not her business, exactly, is it?

BENTLEY. (*returning to the pavilion*) Of course not. Thats why one loves her for doing it. Look here: chuck away your silly weekend novel, and talk to a chap. After a week in that filthy office my brain is simply blue-mouldy. Lets argue about something intellectual. (*He throws himself into the wicker chair on* JOHNNY's *right.*)

JOHNNY. (*straightening up in the swing with a yell of protest*) No. Now seriously, Bunny, Ive come down here to have a pleasant week-end; and I'm not going to stand your confounded arguments. If you want to argue, get out of this and go over to the Congregationalist minister's. He's a nailer at arguing. He likes it.

BENTLEY. You cant argue with a person when his liveli-hood depends on his not letting you convert him. And would you mind not calling me Bunny? My name is Bentley Summerhays, which you please.

JOHNNY. Whats the matter with Bunny?

BENTLEY. It puts me in a false position. Have you ever considered the fact that I was an afterthought?

JOHNNY. An afterthought? What do you mean by that?

BENTLEY. I—

JOHNNY. No, stop: I dont want to know. It's only a dodge to start an argument.

BENTLEY. Dont be afraid: it wont overtax your brain. My father was 44 when I was born. My mother was 41. There was twelve years between me and the next eldest. I was unexpected. I was probably unintentional. My brother and sisters are not the least like me. Theyre the regular thing that you always get in the first batch from young parents: quite pleasant, ordinary, do-the-regular-thing sort: all body and no brains, like you.

JOHNNY. Thank you.

BENTLEY. Dont mention it, old chap. Now I'm differ-ent. By the time I was born, the old couple knew some-thing. So I came out all brains and no more body than is absolutely necessary. I am really a good deal older than you, though you were born ten years sooner. Everybody feels that when they hear us talk; consequently, though it's quite natural to hear me calling you Johnny, it sounds ridiculous and unbecoming for you to call me Bunny. (*He rises*).

JOHNNY. Does it, by George? You stop me doing it if you can: thats all.

BENTLEY. If you go on doing it after Ive asked you not, youll feel an awful swine (*He strolls away carelessly to the sideboard with his eye on the sponge-cakes*) At least I should; but I suppose youre not so particular.

JOHNNY. (*rising vengefully and following* BENTLEY, *who is forced to turn and listen*) I'll tell you what it is, my boy: you want a good talking to; and I'm going to give it to you. If you think that because your father's a K.C.B., and you want to marry my sister, you can make yourself as nasty as you please and say what you like, youre mistaken. Let me tell you that except Hypatia, not one person in this house is in favor of her marrying you; and I dont believe she's happy about it herself. The match isnt settled yet: dont forget that. Youre on trial in the office because the Governor isnt giving his daughter money for an idle man to live on her. Youre on trial here because my mother thinks a girl should know what a man is like in the house before she marries him. Thats been going on for two months now; and whats the result? Youve got yourself thoroughly disliked in the office; and youre getting yourself thoroughly disliked here, all through your bad manners and your conceit, and the damned impudence you think clever.

BENTLEY. (*deeply wounded and trying hard to control himself*) Thats enough, thank you. You dont suppose, I hope, that I should have come down if I had known that that was how you all feel about me. (*He makes for the vestibule door*).

JOHNNY. (*collaring him*) No: you dont run away. I'm going to have this out with you. Sit down: d'y' hear? (BENTLEY *attempts to go with dignity.* JOHNNY *slings him into a chair at the writing table, where he sits, bitterly humiliated, but afraid to speak lest he should burst into tears).* That's the advantage to having more body than brains, you see: it enables me to teach you manners; and I'm going to do it too. Youre a spoilt young pup; and you need a jolly good licking. And if you're not careful youll get it: I'll see to that next time you call me a swine.

BENTLEY. I didnt call you a swine. But *(Bursting into a fury of tears)* you a r e a swine: youre a beast: youre a brute: youre a cad: youre a liar: youre a bully: I should like to wring your damned neck for you.

JOHNNY. *(with a derisive laugh)* Try it, my son. (BENTLEY *gives an inarticulate sob of rage*) Fighting isnt in your line. Youre too small; and youre too childish. I always suspected that your cleverness wouldnt come to very much when it was brought up against something solid: some decent chap's fist, for instance.

BENTLEY. I hope your beastly fist may come up against a mad bull or a prizefighter's nose, or something solider than me. I dont care about your fist; but if everybody here dislikes me— *(He is checked by a sob)* Well, I dont care. *(Trying to recover himself)* I'm sorry I intruded: I didnt know. *(Breaking down again)* Oh you beast! you pig! Swine, swine, swine, swine, swine! Now!

JOHNNY. All right, my lad, all right. Sling your mud as hard as you please: it wont stick to me. What I want to know is this. How is it that your father, who I suppose is the strongest man England has produced in our time—

BENTLEY. You got that out of your halfpenny paper. A lot y o u know about him!

JOHNNY. I dont set up to be able to do anything but admire him and appreciate him and be proud of him as an Englishman. If it wasnt for my respect for him, I wouldnt have stood your cheek for two days, let alone two months. But what I cant understand is why he didnt lick it out of you when you were a kid. For twenty-five years he kept a place twice as big as England in order: a place full of seditious coffee-colored heathens and pestilential white agitators in the middle of a lot of savage tribes. And yet he couldnt keep you in order. I dont set up to be half the man your father undoubtedly is; but, by George, it's lucky for you you were not my son. I dont hold with my own father's views about corporal punishment being wrong. It's necessary for some people; and I'd have tried it on you until you first learnt to howl and then to behave yourself.

BENTLEY. (*contemptuously*) Yes: behavior wouldnt come naturally to your son, would it?

JOHNNY. (*stung into suden violence*) Now you keep a civil tongue in your head. I'll stand none of your snobbery. I'm just as proud of Tarleton's Underwear as you are of your father's title and his K.C.B., and all the rest of it. My father began in a little hole of a shop in Leeds no bigger than our pantry down the passage there. He—

BENTLEY. Oh yes: I know. Ive read it. "The Romance of Business, or The Story of Tarleton's Underwear. Please Take One!" I took one the day after I first met Hypatia. I went and bought half a dozen unshrinkable vests for her sake.

JOHNNY. Well: did they shrink?

BENTLEY. Oh, dont be a fool.

JOHNNY. Never mind whether I'm a fool or not. Did they shrink? Thats the point. Were they worth the money?

BENTLEY. I couldnt wear them: do you think my skin's as thick as your customers' hides? I'd as soon have dressed myself in a nutmeg grater.

JOHNNY. Pity your father didnt give your thin skin a jolly good lacing with a cane!

BENTLEY. Pity you havnt got more than one idea! If you want to know, they did try that on me once, when I was a small kid. A silly governess did it. I yelled fit to bring down the house, and went into convulsions and brain fever and that sort of thing for three weeks. So the old girl got the sack; and serve her right! After that, I was let do what I liked. My father didnt want me to grow up a broken-spirited spaniel, which is your idea of a man, I suppose.

JOHNNY. Jolly good thing for you that m y father made you come into the office and shew what you were made of. And it didnt come to much: let me tell you that. When the Governor asked me where I thought we ought to put you, I said "Make him the Office Boy." The Governor said you were too green. And so you were.

BENTLEY. I daresay. So would you be pretty green if you were shoved into my father's set. I picked up your silly business in a fortnight. Youve been at it ten years; and you havnt picked it up yet.

JOHNNY. Dont talk rot, child. You know you simply make me pity you.

BENTLEY. "Romance of Business" indeed! The real romance of Tarleton's business is the story that you understand anything about it. You never could explain any mortal thing about it to me when I asked you. "See what was done the last time": that was the beginning and the end of your wisdom. Youre nothing but a turnspit.

JOHNNY. A what!

BENTLEY. A turnspit. If your father hadnt made a roasting jack for you to turn, youd be earning twenty-four shillings a week behind a counter.

JOHNNY. If you dont take that back and apologize for your bad manners, I'll give you as good a hiding as ever—

BENTLEY. Help! Johnny's beating me! Oh! Murder! (*He throws himself on the ground, uttering piercing yells*).

JOHNNY. Dont be a fool. Stop that noise, will you, I'm not going to touch you. Sh— Sh—

HYPATIA *rushes in through the inner door, followed by* MRS TARLETON, *and throws herself on her knees by* BENTLEY. MRS TARLETON, *whose knees are stiffer, bends over him and tries to lift him.* MRS TARLETON *is a shrewd and motherly old lady who has been pretty in her time, and is still very pleasant and likeable and unaffected.*

HYPATIA *is a typical English girl of a sort never called typical: that is, she has an opaque white skin, black hair, large dark eyes with black brows and lashes, curved lips, swift glances and movements that flash out of a waving stillness, boundless energy and audacity held in leash.*

HYPATIA. (*pounding on* BENTLEY *with no very gentle hand*) Bentley: whats the matter? Dont cry like that: whats the use? Whats happened?

MRS TARLETON. Are you ill, child? (*They get him up*) There, there, pet! It's all right: dont cry (*They put him into a chair*): there! there! there! Johnny will go for the doctor; and he'll give you something nice to make it well.

HYPATIA. What has happened, Johnny?

MRS TARLETON. Was it a wasp?

BENTLEY. (*impatiently*) Wasp be dashed!

MRS TARLETON. Oh Bunny! that was a naughty word.

BENTLEY. Yes, I know: I beg your pardon. (*He rises, and extricates himself from them*) Thats all right. Johnny frightened me. You know how easy it is to hurt me; and I'm too small to defend myself against Johnny.

MRS TARLETON. Johnny: how often have I told you that you must not bully the little ones. I thought youd outgrown all that.

HYPATIA. (*angrily*) I do declare, mamma, that Johnny's brutality makes it impossible to live in the house with him.

JOHNNY. (*deeply hurt*) It's fourteen years, mother, since you had that row with me for licking Robert and giving Hypatia a black eye because she bit me. I promised you then that I'd never raise my hand to one of them again; and Ive never broken my word. And now because this young whelp begins to cry out before he's hurt, you treat me as if I were a brute and a savage.

MRS TARLETON. No dear, not a savage; but you know you mustnt call our visitor naughty names.

BENTLEY. Oh, let him alone—

JOHNNY. (*fiercely*) Dont you interfere between my mother and me: d'y' hear?

HYPATIA. Johnny's lost his temper, mother. We'd better go. Come, Bentley.

MRS TARLETON. Yes: that will be best. (*To* BENTLEY) Johnny doesnt mean any harm, dear: he'll be himself presently. Come.

The two ladies go out through the inner door with BENTLEY, *who turns derisively at the door to cock a snook at* JOHNNY *as he goes out.* JOHNNY, *left alone, clenches his fists and grinds his teeth, but can find no relief in that way for his rage. After choking and stamping for a moment, he makes for the vestibule door. It opens before he reaches it; and* LORD SUMMERHAYS *comes in.* JOHNNY *glares at him, speechless.* LORD SUMMERHAYS *takes in the situation, and quickly takes the punchbowl from the sideboard and offers it to* JOHNNY.

LORD SUMMERHAYS. Smash it. Dont hesitate: it's an ugly thing. Smash it: hard. (JOHNNY, *with a stifled yell, dashes it in pieces, and then sits down and mops his brow*) Feel better now? (JOHNNY *nods.*) I know only one person alive who could drive me to the point of having either to break china or commit murder; and that person is my son Bentley. Was it he? (JOHNNY *nods again, not yet able to speak*) As the car stopped I heard a yell which is only too familiar to me. It generally means that some infuriated person is trying to thrash Bentley. Nobody has ever succeeded, though almost everybody has tried. (*He seats himself comfortably close to the writing table, and sets to work to collect the fragments of the punchbowl in the waste-paper basket whilst* JOHNNY, *with diminishing difficulty, collects himself*) Bentley is a problem which I confess I have never been able to solve. He was born to be a great success at the age of fifty. Most Englishmen of his class seem to be born to be great successes at the age of twenty-four at

most. The domestic problem for me is how to endure
Bentley until he is fifty. The problem for the nation is
how to get itself governed by men whose growth is ar-
rested when they are little more than college lads.
Bentley doesnt really mean to be offensive. You can always make him cry by telling him you dont like him.
Only, he cries so loud that the experiment should be made
in the open air: in the middle of Salisbury Plain if possible. He has a hard and penetrating intellect and a remarkable power of looking facts in the face; but unfortunately, being very young, he has no idea of how very
little of that sort of thing most of us can stand. On the
other hand, he is frightfully sensitive and even affectionate; so that he probably gets as much as he gives in
the way of hurt feelings. Youll excuse me rambling on
like this about my son.

JOHNNY. (*who has pulled himself together*) You did
it on purpose. I wasnt quite myself: I needed a moment
to pull round. Thank you.

LORD SUMMERHAYS. Not at all. Is your father at home?

JOHNNY. No: he's opening one of his free libraries.
Thats another nice little penny gone. He's mad on reading. He promised another free library last week. It's
ruinous. Itll hit you as well as me when Bunny marries
Hypatia. When all Hypatia's money is thrown away on
libraries, where will Bunny come in? Cant you stop him?

LORD SUMMERHAYS. I'm afraid not. He's a perfect
whirlwind. Indefatigable at public work. Wonderful man,
I think.

JOHNNY. Oh, public work! He does too much of it. It's
really a sort of laziness, getting away from your own
serious business to amuse yourself with other people's.
Mind: I dont say there isnt another side to it. It has its
value as an advertisement. It makes useful acquaintances
and leads to valuable business connections. But it takes
his mind off the main chance; and he overdoes it.

LORD SUMMERHAYS. The danger of public business is
that it never ends. A man may kill himself at it.

JOHNNY. Or he can spend more on it than it brings him in: thats how I look at it. What I say is that everybody's business is nobody's business. I hope I'm not a hard man, nor a narrow man, nor unwilling to pay reasonable taxes, and subscribe in reason to deserving charities, and even serve on a jury in my turn; and no man can say I ever refused to help a friend out of a difficulty when he was worth helping. But when you ask me to go beyond that, I tell you frankly I dont see it. I never did see it, even when I was only a boy, and had to pretend to take in all the ideas the Governor fed me up with. I didnt see it; and I dont see it.

LORD SUMMERHAYS. There is certainly no business reason why you should take more than your share of the world's work.

JOHNNY. So I say. It's really a great encouragement to me to find you agree with me. For of course if nobody agrees with you, how are you to know that youre not a fool?

LORD SUMMERHAYS. Quite so.

JOHNNY. I wish youd talk to him about it. It's no use my saying anything: I'm a child to him still: I have no influence. Besides, you know how to handle men. See how you handled me when I was making a fool of myself about Bunny!

LORD SUMMERHAYS. Not at all.

JOHNNY. Oh yes I was: I know I was. Well, if my blessed father had come in he'd have told me to control myself. As if I was losing my temper on purpose!

BENTLEY *returns, newly washed. He beams when he sees his father, and comes affectionately behind him and pats him on the shoulders.*

BENTLEY. Hel-lo, commander! have you come? Ive been making a filthy silly ass of myself here. I'm awfully sorry, Johnny, old chap: I beg your pardon. Why dont you kick me when I go on like that?

LORD SUMMERHAYS. As we came through Godalming I thought I heard some yelling—

BENTLEY. I should think you did. Johnny was rather rough on me, though. He told me nobody here liked me; and I was silly enough to believe him.

LORD SUMMERHAYS. And all the women have been kissing you and pitying you ever since to stop your crying, I suppose. Baby!

BENTLEY. I did cry. But I always feel good after crying: it relieves my wretched nerves. I feel perfectly jolly now.

LORD SUMMERHAYS. Not at all ashamed of yourself, for instance?

BENTLEY. If I started being ashamed of myself I shouldnt have time for anything else all my life. I say: I feel very fit and spry. Lets all go down and meet the Grand Cham. (*He goes to the hat stand and takes down his hat*).

LORD SUMMERHAYS. Does Mr Tarleton like to be called the Grand Cham, do you think, Bentley?

BENTLEY. Well, he thinks he's too modest for it. He calls himself Plain John. But you cant call him that in his own office: besides, it doesnt suit him: it's not flamboyant enough.

JOHNNY. Flam what?

BENTLEY. Flamboyant. Lets go and meet him. He's telephoned from Guildford to say he's on the road. The dear old son is always telephoning or telegraphing: he thinks he's hustling along like anything when he's only sending unnecessary messages.

LORD SUMMERHAYS. Thank you: I should prefer a quiet afternoon.

BENTLEY. Righto! I shant press Johnny: he's had enough of me for one week-end. (*He goes out through the pavilion into the grounds*).

JOHNNY. Not a bad idea, that.

LORD SUMMERHAYS. What?

JOHNNY. Going to meet the Governor. You know you wouldn't think it; but the Governor likes Bunny rather. And Bunny is cultivating it. I shouldnt be surprised if he thought he could squeeze me out one of these days.

LORD SUMMERHAYS. You dont say so! Young rascal! I want to consult you about him, if you dont mind. Shall we stroll over to the Gibbet? Bentley is too fast for me as a walking companion; but I should like a short turn.

JOHNNY. (*rising eagerly, highly flattered*) Right you are. Thatll suit me down to the ground. (*He takes a Panama and stick from the hat stand*).

MRS TARLETON *and* HYPATIA *come back just as the two men are going out.* HYPATIA *salutes* SUMMERHAYS *from a distance with an enigmatic lift of her eyelids in his direction and a demure nod before she sits down at the worktable and busies herself with her needle.* MRS TARLETON, *hospitably fussy, goes over to him.*

MRS TARLETON. Oh, Lord Summerhays, I didnt know you were here. Wont you have some tea?

LORD SUMMERHAYS. No, thank you: I'm not allowed tea. And I'm ashamed to say Ive knocked over your beautiful punchbowl. You must let me replace it.

MRS TARLETON. Oh, it doesnt matter: I'm only too glad to be rid of it. The shopman told me it was in the best taste; but when my poor old nurse Martha got cataract, Bunny said it was a merciful provision of Nature to prevent her seeing our china.

LORD SUMMERHAYS. (*gravely*) That was exceedingly rude of Bentley, Mrs Tarleton. I hope you told him so.

MRS TARLETON. Oh, bless you! I dont care what he says; so long as he says it to me and not before visitors.

JOHNNY. We're going out for a stroll, mother.

MRS TARLETON. All right: dont let us keep you. Never mind about the crock: I'll get the girl to come and take the pieces away. (*Recollecting herself*) There! Ive done it again!

JOHNNY. Done what?

MRS TARLETON. Called her the girl. You know, Lord Summerhays, it's a funny thing; but now I'm getting old, I'm dropping back into all the ways John and I had when we had barely a hundred a year. You should have known me when I was forty! I talked like a duchess; and if Johnny or Hypatia let slip a word that was like old times, I was down on them like anything. And now I'm beginning to do it myself at every turn.

LORD SUMMERHAYS. There comes a time when all that seems to matter so little. Even queens drop the mask when they reach our time of life.

MRS TARLETON. Let you alone for giving a thing a pretty turn! Youre a humbug, you know, Lord Summerhays. John doesnt know it; and Johnny doesnt know it; but you and I know it, dont we? Now thats something that even you cant answer; so be off with you for your walk without another word.

LORD SUMMERHAYS *smiles; bows; and goes out through the vestibule door, followed by* JOHNNY. MRS TARLETON *sits down at the worktable and takes out her darning materials and one of her husband's socks.* HYPATIA *is at the other side of the table, on her mother's right. They chat as they work.*

HYPATIA. I wonder whether they laugh at us when they are by themselves!

MRS TARLETON. Who?

HYPATIA. Bentley and his father and all the toffs in their set.

MRS TARLETON. Oh, thats only their way. I used to think that the aristocracy were a nasty sneering lot, and that they were laughing at me and John. Theyre always giggling and pretending not to care much about anything. But you get used to it: theyre the same to one another and to everybody. Besides, what does it matter what they think? It's far worse when theyre civil, because that always means that they want you to lend them money; and

you must never do that, Hypatia, because they never pay.
How can they? They dont make anything, you see. Of
course, if you can make up your mind to regard it as a
gift, thats different; but then they generally ask you
again; and you may as well say no first as last. You
neednt be afraid of the aristocracy, dear: theyre only
human creatures like ourselves after all; and youll hold
your own with them easy enough.

HYPATIA. Oh, I'm not a bit afraid of them, I assure
you.

MRS TARLETON. Well, no, not afraid of them, exactly;
but youve got to pick up their ways. You know, dear,
I never quite agreed with your father's notion of keeping
clear of them, and sending you to a school that was so
expensive that they couldnt afford to send their daughters
there; so that all the girls belonged to big business families
like ourselves. It takes all sorts to make a world; and I
wanted you to see a little of all sorts. When you marry
Bunny, and go among the women of his father's set, theyll
shock you at first.

HYPATIA. (*incredulously*) How?

MRS TARLETON. Well, the things they talk about.

HYPATIA. Oh! scandalmongering?

MRS TARLETON. Oh no: we all do that: thats only
human nature. But you know theyve no notion of
decency. I shall never forget the first day I spent with
a marchioness, two duchesses, and no end of Ladies This
and That. Of course it was only a committee: theyd put
me on to get a big subscription out of John. I'd never
heard such talk in my life. The things they mentioned!
And it was the marchioness that started it.

HYPATIA. What sort of things?

MRS TARLETON. Drainage!! She'd tried three systems
in her castle; and she was going to do away with them
all and try another. I didnt know which way to look when
she began talking about it: I thought theyd all have got
up and gone out of the room. But not a bit of it, if you

please. They were all just as bad as she. They all had systems; and each of them swore by her own system. I sat there with my cheeks burning until one of the duchesses, thinking I looked out of it, I suppose, asked me what system I had. I said I was sure I knew nothing about such things, and hadnt we better change the subject. Then the fat was in the fire, I can tell you. There was a regular terror of a countess with an anaerobic system; and she told me, downright brutally, that I'd better learn something about them before my children died of diphtheria. That was just two months after I'd buried poor little Bobby; and that was the very thing he died of, poor little lamb! I burst out crying: I couldnt help it. It was as good as telling me I'd killed by own child. I had to go away; but before I was out of the door one of the duchesses—quite a young woman—began talking about what sour milk did in her inside and how she expected to live to be over a hundred if she took it regularly. And me listening to her, that had never dared to think that a duchess could have anything so common as an inside! I shouldnt have minded if it had been children's insides: we h a v e to talk about them. But grown-up people! I w a s glad to get away that time.

HYPATIA. There was a physiology and hygiene class started at school; but of course none of our girls were let attend it.

MRS TARLETON. If it had been an aristocratic school plenty would have attended it. Thats what theyre like: theyve nasty minds. With really nice good women a thing is either decent or indecent; and if it's indecent, we just dont mention it or pretend to know about it; and theres an end of it. But all the aristocracy cares about is whether it can get any good out of the thing. Theyre what Johnny calls cynical-like. And of course nobody can say a word to them for it. Theyre so high up that they can do and say what they like.

HYPATIA. Well, I think they might leave the drains

to their husbands. I shouldn't think much of a man that left such things to me.

MRS TARLETON. Oh, dont think that, dear, whatever you do. I never let on about it to you; but it's me that takes care of the drainage here. After what that countess said to me I wasnt going to lose another child nor trust John. And I dont want my grandchildren to die any more than my children.

HYPATIA. Do you think Bentley will ever be as big a man as his father? I dont mean clever: I mean big and strong.

MRS TARLETON. Not he. He's overbred, like one of those expensive little dogs. I like a bit of a mongrel myself, whether it's a man or a dog; theyre the best for everyday. But we all have our tastes: whats one woman's meat is another woman's poison. Bunny's a dear little fellow; but I never could have fancied him for a husband when I was your age.

HYPATIA. Yes; but he has some brains. He's not like all the rest. One cant have everything.

MRS TARLETON. Oh, youre quite right, dear: quite right. It's a great thing to have brains: look what it's done for your father! Thats the reason I never said a word when you jilted poor Jerry Mackintosh.

HYPATIA. (*excusing herself*) I really couldnt stick it out with Jerry, mother. I know you liked him, and nobody can deny that he's a splendid animal—

MRS TARLETON. (*shocked*) Hypatia! How can you! The things that girls say nowadays!

HYPATIA. Well, what else can you call him? If I'd been deaf or he'd been dumb, I could have married him. But living with father, Ive got accustomed to cleverness. Jerry would drive me mad: you know very well he's a fool: even Johnny thinks him a fool.

MRS TARLETON. (*up in arms at once in defence of her boy*) Now dont begin about my Johnny. You know it annoys me. Johnny's as clever as anybody else in his own way. I dont say he's as clever as you in some ways; but he's a man, at all events, and not a little squit of a thing like your Bunny.

HYPATIA. Oh, I say nothing against your darling: we all know Johnny's perfection.

MRS TARLETON. Don't be cross, dearie. You let Johnny alone; and I'll let Bunny alone. I'm just as bad as you. There!

HYPATIA. Oh, I dont mind your saying that about Bentley. It's true. He i s a squit of a thing. I wish he wasnt. But who else is there? Think of all the other chances Ive had! Not one of them has as much brains in his whole body as Bentley has in his little finger. Besides, theyve no d i s t i n c t i o n. It's as much as I can do to tell one from the other. They wouldn't even have money if they werent the sons of their fathers, like Johnny. Whats a girl to do? I never met anybody like Bentley before. He may be small; but he's the best of the bunch: you cant deny that.

MRS TARLETON. (*with a sigh*) Well, my pet, if you fancy him, theres no more to be said.

A pause follows this remark: the two women sewing silently.

HYPATIA. Mother: do you think marriage is as much a question of fancy as it used to be in your time and father's?

MRS TARLETON. Oh, it wasn't much fancy with me, dear: your father just wouldnt take no for an answer; and I was only too glad to be his wife instead of his shop-girl. Still, it's curious; but I had more choice than you in a way, because, you see, I was poor; and there are so many more poor men than rich ones that I might have had more of a pick, as you might say, if John hadnt suited me.

HYPATIA. I can imagine all sorts of men I could fall in love with; but I never seem to meet them. The real ones are too small, like Bunny, or too silly, like Jerry. Of course one can get into a state about any man: fall in love with him if you like to call it that. But who would risk marrying a man for love? *I* shouldnt. I remember three girls at school who agreed that the one man you should never marry was the man you were in love with, because it would make a perfect slave of you. Theres a sort of instinct against it, I think, thats just as strong as the other instinct. One of them, to my certain knowledge, refused a man she was in love with, and married another who was in love with her, and it turned out very well.

MRS TARLETON. Does all that mean that youre not in love with Bunny?

HYPATIA. Oh, how could anybody be in love with Bunny? I like him to kiss me just as I like a baby to kiss me. I'm fond of him; and he never bores me; and I see that he's very clever; but I'm not what you call gone about him, if thats what you mean.

MRS TARLETON. Then why need you marry him?

HYPATIA. What better can I do? I must marry some-body, I suppose. Ive realized that since I was twenty-three. I always used to take it as a matter of course that I should be married before I was twenty.

BENTLEY'S VOICE. (*in the garden*) Youve got to keep yourself fresh: to look at these things with an open mind.

JOHN TARLETON'S VOICE. Quite right, quite right: I always say so.

MRS TARLETON. Theres your father, and Bunny with him.

BENTLEY. Keep young. Keep your eye on me. Thats the tip for you.

BENTLEY *and* MR TARLETON [*an immense and genial veteran of trade*] *come into view and enter the pavilion.*

JOHN TARLETON. You think youre young, do you? You think I'm old? (*energetically shaking off his motoring coat and hanging it up with his cap*).

BENTLEY. (*helping him with the coat*) Of course youre old. Look at your face and look at mine. What you call your youth is nothing but your levity. Why do we get on so well together? Because I'm a young cub and youre an old josser. (*He throws a cushion at* HYPATIA'S *feet and sits down on it with his back against her knees*).

TARLETON. Old! Thats all you know about it, my lad. How do, Patsy! (HYPATIA *kisses him*) How is my Chickabiddy? (*He kisses* MRS TARLETON'S *hand and poses expansively in the middle of the picture*) Look at me! Look at these wrinkles, these grey hairs, this repulsive mask that you call old age! What is it? (*Vehemently*) I ask you, what is it?

BENTLEY. Jolly nice and venerable, old man. Dont be discouraged.

TARLETON. Nice? Not a bit of it. Venerable? Venerable be blowed! Read your Darwin, my boy. Read your Weismann. (*He goes to the sideboard for a drink of lemonade*).

MRS TARLETON. For shame, John! Tell him to read his Bible.

TARLETON. (*manipulating the syphon*) Whats the use of telling children to read the Bible when you know they wont. I was kept away from the Bible for forty years by being told to read it when I was young. Then I picked it up one evening in a hotel in Sunderland when I had left all my papers in the train; and I found its wasnt half bad. (*He drinks, and puts down the glass with a smack of enjoyment*) Better than most halfpenny papers, anyhow, if only you could make people believe it. (*He sits down by the writing table, near his wife*) But if you want to understand old age scientifically, read Darwin and Weismann. Of course if you want to understand it romantically, read about Solomon.

MRS TARLETON. Have you had tea, John?

TARLETON. Yes. Dont interrupt me when I'm improving the boy's mind. Where was I? This repulsive mask— yes. (*Explosively*) What is death?

MRS TARLETON. John!

HYPATIA. Death is a rather unpleasant subject, papa.

TARLETON. Not a bit. Not scientifically. Scientifically

it's a delightful subject. You think death's natural. Well,
it isnt. You read Weismann. There wasnt any death to
start with. You go look in any ditch outside and youll
find swimming about there as fresh as paint some of the
identical little live cells that Adam christened in the
Garden of Eden. But if big things like us didnt die, we'd
crowd one another off the face of the globe. Nothing sur-
vived, sir, except the sort of people that had the sense and
good manners to die and make room for the fresh supplies. And so death was introduced by Natural Selection.
You get it out of your head, my lad, that I'm going to
die because I'm wearing out or decaying. Theres no such
thing as decay to a vital man. I shall clear out; but I
shant decay.

BENTLEY. And what about the wrinkles and the almond
tree and the grasshopper that becomes a burden and the
desire that fails?

TARLETON. Does it? by George! No, sir: it spiritualizes.
As to your grasshopper, I can carry an elephant.

MRS TARLETON. You do say such things, Bunny!
What does he mean by the almond tree?

TARLETON. He means my white hairs: the repulsive
mask. That, my boy, is another invention of Natural
Selection to disgust young women with me, and give the
lads a turn.

MRS TARLETON. John: I wont have it. Thats a forbidden subject.

TARLETON. They talk of the wickedness and vanity of
women painting their faces and wearing auburn wigs at
fifty. But why shouldnt they? Why should a woman allow
Nature to put a false mask of age on her when she knows
that she's as young as ever? Why should she look in the
glass and see a wrinkled lie when a touch of fine art will
shew her a glorious truth? The wrinkles are a dodge to
repel young men. Suppose she doesnt want to repel young
men! Suppose she likes them!

MRS TARLETON. Bunny: take Hypatia out into the

grounds for a walk: theres a good boy. John has got one of his naughty fits this evening.

HYPATIA. Oh, never mind me. I'm used to him.

BENTLEY. I'm not. I never heard such conversation: I cant believe my ears. And mind you, this is the man who objected to my marrying his daughter on the ground that a marriage between a member of the great and good middle class with one of the vicious and corrupt aristocracy would be a misalliance. A misalliance, if you please! This is the man Ive adopted as a father!

TARLETON. Eh? Whats that? Adopted me as a father, have you?

BENTLEY. Yes. Thats an idea of mine, I knew a chap named Joey Percival at Oxford (you know I was two months at Balliol before I was sent down for telling the old woman who was head of that silly college what I jolly well thought of him. He would have been glad to have me back, too, at the end of six months; but I wouldnt go: I just let him want; and serve him right!) Well, Joey was a most awfully clever fellow, and so nice! I asked him what made such a difference between him and all the other pups—they w e r e pups, if you like. He told be it was very simple: they had only one father apiece; and he had three.

MRS TARLETON. Dont talk nonsense, child. How could that be?

BENTLEY. Oh, very simple. His father—

TARLETON. Which father?

BENTLEY. The first one: the regulation natural chap. He kept a tame philosopher in the house; a sort of Coleridge or Herbert Spencer kind of card, you know. That was the second father. Then his mother was an Italian princess; and she had an Italian priest always about. He was supposed to take charge of her conscience; but from what I could make out she jolly well took charge of his. The whole three of them took charge of Joey's conscience. He used to hear them arguing like mad about everything. You see, the philosopher was a freethinker, and always believed the latest thing. The priest didnt believe anything, because it was sure to get him into trouble with someone or another. And the natural father kept an open mind and believed whatever paid him best. Between the lot of them Joey got cultivated no end. He said if he could only have had three mothers as well, he'd have backed himself against Napoleon.

TARLETON. (*impressed*) Thats an idea. Thats a most interesting idea: a most important idea.

MRS TARLETON. You always were one for ideas, John.

TARLETON. Youre right, Chickabiddy. What do I tell Johnny when he brags about Tarleton's Underwear? It's not the underwear. The underwear be hanged! Anybody can make underwear. Anybody can sell underwear. Tarleton's Ideas: thats whats done it. Ive often thought of putting that up over the shop.

BENTLEY. Take me into partnership when you do, old man. I'm wasted on the underwear; but I shall come in strong on the ideas.

TARLETON. You be a good boy; and perhaps I will.

MRS TARLETON. (*scenting a plot against her beloved* JOHNNY) Now, John: you promised—

TARLETON. Yes, yes. All right, Chickabiddy: don't fuss. Your precious Johnny shant be interfered with. (*Bouncing up, too energetic to sit still*) But I'm getting sick of that old shop. Thirty-five years Ive had of it: same blessed old stairs to go up and down every day: same old lot: same old game: sorry I ever started it now. I'll chuck it and try something else: something that will give a scope to all my faculties.

HYPATIA. Theres money in underwear: theres none in wild-cat ideas.

TARLETON. Theres money in m e, madam, no matter what I go into.

MRS TARLETON. Dont boast, John. Dont tempt Providence.

TARLETON. Rats! You dont understand Providence. Providence likes to be tempted. Thats the secret of the successful man. Read Browning. Natural theology on an island, eh? Caliban was afraid to tempt Providence: that was why he was never able to get even with Prospero. What did Prospero do? Prospero didnt even tempt Providence: he w a s Providence. Thats one of Tarleton's ideas; and dont you forget it.

BENTLEY. You a r e full of beef today, old man.

TARLETON. Beef be blowed! Joy of life. Read Ibsen. (*He goes into the pavilion to relieve his restlessness, and stares out with his hands thrust deep in his pockets*).

HYPATIA. (*thoughtful*) Bentley: couldnt you invite your friend Mr Percival down here?

BENTLEY. Not if I know it. Youd throw me over the moment you set eyes on him.

MRS TARLETON. Oh, Bunny! For shame!

BENTLEY. Well, who'd marry me, dyou suppose, if they could get my brains with a full-sized body? No, thank you. I shall take jolly good care to keep Joey out of this until Hypatia is past praying for.

JOHNNY *and* LORD SUMMERHAYS *return through the pavilion from their stroll*.

TARLETON. Welcome! welcome! Why have you stayed away so long?

LORD SUMMERHAYS. (*shaking hands*) Yes: I should have come sooner. But I'm still rather lost in England. (JOHNNY *takes his hat and hangs it up beside his own*) Thank you. (JOHNNY *returns to his swing and his novel.* LORD SUMMERHAYS *comes to the writing table*) The fact is that as Ive nothing to do, I never have time to go anywhere. (*He sits down next* MRS TARLETON).

TARLETON. (*following him and sitting down on his left*) Paradox, paradox. Good. Paradoxes are the only truths. Read Chesterton. But theres lots for you to do here. You have a genius for government. You learnt your job out there in Jinghiskahn. Well, we want to be governed here in England. Govern us.

LORD SUMMERHAYS. Ah yes, my friend; but in Jinghiskahn you have to govern the right way. If you dont, you go under and come home. Here everything has to be done the wrong way, to suit governors who understand nothing but partridge shooting (our English native princes, in fact) and voters who dont know what theyre voting about. I dont understand these democratic games; and I'm afraid I'm too old to learn. What can I do but sit in the window of my club, which consists mostly of retired Indian Civil servants? We look on at the muddle and the folly and amateurishness; and we ask each other where a single fortnight of it would have landed us.

TARLETON. Very true. Still, Democracy's all right, you know. Read Mill. Read Jefferson.

LORD SUMMERHAYS. Yes. Democracy reads well; but it doesnt act well, like some people's plays. No, no, my friend Tarleton: to make Democracy work, you need an aristocratic democracy. To make Aristocracy work, you need a democratic aristocracy. Youve got neither, and theres an end of it.

TARLETON. Still, you know, the superman may come. The superman's an idea. I believe in ideas. Read Whatshisname.

LORD SUMMERHAYS. Reading is a dangerous amusement, Tarleton. I wish I could persuade your free library people of that.

TARLETON. Why man, it's the beginning of education.

LORD SUMMERHAYS. On the contrary, it's the end of it. How can you dare teach a man to read until youve taught him everything else first?

JOHNNY. (*intercepting his father's reply by coming out of the swing and taking the floor*) Leave it at that. Thats good sense. Anybody on for a game of tennis?

BENTLEY. Oh, lets have some more improving conversation. Wouldnt you rather, Johnny?

JOHNNY. If you ask me, no.

TARLETON. Johnny: you dont cultivate your mind. Y o u dont read.

JOHNNY. (*coming between his mother and* LORD SUM-MERHAYS, *book in hand*) Yes I do. I bet you what you like that, page for page, I read more than you, though I dont talk about it so much. Only, I don't read the same books. I like a book with a plot in it. You like a book with nothing in it but some idea that the chap that writes it keeps worrying, like a cat chasing its own tail. I can stand a little of it, just as I can stand watching the cat for two minutes, say, when Ive nothing better to do. But a man soon gets fed up with that sort of thing. The fact is, you look on an author as a sort of god. *I* look on him as a man that I pay to do a certain thing for me. I pay him to amuse me and to take me out of myself and make me forget.

TARLETON. No. Wrong principle. You want to remember. Read Kipling. "Lest we forget."

JOHNNY. If Kipling wants to remember, let him remember. If he had to run Tarleton's Underwear, he'd be jolly glad to forget. As he has a much softer job, and wants to keep himself before the public, his cry is, "Dont you forget the sort of things I'm rather clever at writing about." Well, I dont blame him: it's his business: I should do the same in his place. But what he wants and what I want are two different things. I want to forget; and I pay another man to make me forget. If I buy a book or go to the theatre, I want to forget the shop and forget myself from the moment I go in to the moment I come out. Thats what I pay my money for. And if I find that the author's simply getting at me the whole time, I consider that he's obtained my money under false pretences. I'm not a morbid crank: I'm a natural man; and, as such, I dont like being got at. If a man in my employment did it, I should sack him. If a member of my club did it, I should cut him. If he went too far with it, I should bring his conduct before the committee. I might even punch his head, if it came to that. Well, who and what is an author that he should be privileged to take liberties that are not allowed to other men?

MRS TARLETON. You see, John! What have I always told you? Johnny has as much to say for himself as anybody when he likes.

JOHNNY. I'm no fool, mother, whatever some people may fancy. I dont set up to have as many ideas as the governor; but what ideas I have are consecutive, at all events. I can think as well as talk.

BENTLEY. (*to* TARLETON, *chuckling*) Had you there, old man, hadnt he? You a r e rather all over the shop with your ideas, aint you?

JOHNNY. (*handsomely*) I'm not saying anything against you, governor. But I do say that the time has come for sane, healthy, unpretending men like me to make a stand against this conspiracy of the writing and talking and artistic lot to put us in the back row. It isnt a fact that we're inferior to them: it's a put-up job; and it's they that have put the job up. It's we that run the country for them; and all the thanks we get is to be told we're Philistines and vulgar tradesmen and sordid city men and so forth, and that theyre all angels of light and leading. The time has come to assert ourselves and put a stop to their stuck-up nonsense. Perhaps if we had nothing better to do than talking or writing, we could do it better than they. Anyhow, theyre the failures and refuse of business (hardly a man of them that didnt begin in an office) and we're the successes of it. Thank God I havnt failed yet at anything; and I dont believe I should fail at literature if it would pay me to turn my hand to it.

BENTLEY. Hear, hear!

MRS TARLETON. Fancy you writing a book, Johnny! Do you think he could, Lord Summerhays?

LORD SUMMERHAYS. Why not? As a matter of fact all the really prosperous authors I have met since my return to England have been very like him.

TARLETON. (*again impressed*) Thats an idea. Thats a new idea. I believe I ought to have made Johnny an author. Ive never said so before for fear of hurting his feelings, because, after all, the lad cant help it; but Ive never thought Johnny worth tuppence as a man of business.

JOHNNY. (*sarcastic*) Oh! You think youve always kept that to yourself, do you, Governor? I know your opinion of me as well as you know it yourself. It takes one man of business to appreciate another; and you arnt, and you never have been, a real man of business. I know where Tarleton's would have been three or four times if it hadnt been for me. (*With a snort and a nod to emphasize the implied warning, he retreats to the Turkish bath, and lolls against it with an air of good-humored indifference*).

TARLETON. Well, who denies it? Youre quite right, my boy. I dont mind confessing to you all that the circumstances that condemned me to keep a shop are the biggest tragedy in modern life. I ought to have been a writer. I'm essentially a man of ideas. When I was a young man I sometimes used to pray that I might fail, so that I should be justified in giving up business and doing something: something first-class. But it was no good: I couldnt fail. I said to myself that if I could only once go to my Chickabiddy here and shew her a chartered accountant's statement proving that I'd made £20 less than last year, I could ask her to let me chance Johnny's and Hypatia's future by going into literature. But it was no good. First it was £250 more than last year. Then it was £700. Then it was £2000. Then I saw it was no use: Prometheus was chained to his rock: read Shelley: read Mrs Browning. Well, well, it was not to be. (*He rises solemnly*) Lord Summerhays: I ask you to excuse me for a few moments. There are times when a man needs to meditate in solitude on his destiny. A chord is touched; and he sees the drama of his life as a spectator sees a play. Laugh if you feel inclined: no man sees the comic side of it more than I. In the theatre of life everyone may be amused except the actor. (*Brightening*) Theres an idea in this: an idea for a picture. What a pity young Bentley is not a painter! Tarleton meditating on his destiny. Not in a toga. Not in the trappings of the tragedian or the philosopher. In plain coat and trousers: a man like any other man. And beneath that coat and trousers a human soul. Tarleton's Underwear! (*He goes out gravely into the vestibule*).

MRS TARLETON. (*fondly*) I suppose it's a wife's partiality, Lord Summerhays; but I do think John is really great. I'm sure he was meant to be a king. My father looked down on John, because he was a rate collector and John kept a shop. It hurt his pride to have to borrow money so often from John; and he used to console himself by saying, "After all, he's only a linendraper." But at last one day he said to me, "John is a king."

BENTLEY. How much did he borrow on that occasion?

LORD SUMMERHAYS. (*sharply*) Bentley!

MRS TARLETON. Oh, don't scold the child: he'd have to say something like that if it was to be his last word on earth. Besides, he's quite right: my poor father had asked for his usual five pounds; and John gave him a hundred in his big way. Just like a king.

LORD SUMMERHAYS. Not at all. I had five kings to manage in Jinghiskahn; and I think you do your husband some injustice, Mrs Tarleton. They pretended to like me because I kept their brothers from murdering them; but I didnt like them. And I like Tarleton.

MRS TARLETON. Everybody does. I really must go and make the cook do him a Welsh rabbit. He expects one on special occasions. (*She goes to the inner door*) Johnny: when he comes back ask him where we're to put that new Turkish bath. Turkish baths are his latest. (*She goes out*).

JOHNNY. (*coming forward again*) Now that the governor has given himself away, and the old lady's gone, I'll tell you something, Lord Summerhays. If you study men whove made an enormous pile in business without being keen on money, youll find that they all have a slate off. The governor's a wonderful man; but he's not quite all there, you know. If you notice, he's different from me; and whatever my failings may be, I'm a sane man. Erratic: thats what he is. And the danger is that some day he'll give the whole show away.

LORD SUMMERHAYS. Giving the show away is a method like any other method. Keeping it to yourself is only another method. I should keep an open mind about it.

JOHNNY. Has it ever occurred to you that a man with an open mind must be a bit of a scoundrel? If you ask me, I like a man who makes up his mind once for all as to whats right and whats wrong and then sticks to it. At all events you know where to have him.

LORD SUMMERHAYS. That may not be his object.

BENTLEY. He may want to have y o u old chap.

JOHNNY. Well, let him. If a member of my club wants to steal my umbrella, he knows where to find it. If a man put up for the club who had an open mind on the subject of property in umbrellas, I should blackball him. An open mind is all very well in clever talky-talky; but in conduct and in business give me solid ground.

LORD SUMMERHAYS. Yes: the quicksands make life difficult. Still, there they are. It's no use pretending theyre rocks.

JOHNNY. I dont know. You can draw a line and make other chaps toe it. Thats what I call morality.

LORD SUMMERHAYS. Very true. But you dont make any progress when youre toeing a line.

HYPATIA. (*suddenly, as if she could bear no more of it*) Bentley: do go and play tennis with Johnny. You must take exercise.

LORD SUMMERHAYS. Do, my boy, do. (*To* JOHNNY) Take him out and make him skip about.

BENTLEY. (*rising reluctantly*) I promised you two inches more round my chest this summer. I tried exercises with an indiarubber expander; but I wasnt strong enough: instead of m y expanding i t, i t crumpled m e up. Come along, Johnny.

JOHNNY. Do you no end of good, young chap. (*He goes out with* BENTLEY *through the pavilion*).

HYPATIA *throws aside her work with an enormous sigh of relief.*

LORD SUMMERHAYS. At last!

HYPATIA. At last. Oh, if I might only have a holiday in an asylum for the dumb. How I envy the animals! They cant talk. If Johnny could only put back his ears or wag his tail instead of laying down the law, how much better it would be! We should know when he was cross and when he was pleased; and thats all we know now, with all his talk. It never stops: talk, talk, talk, talk. Thats my life. All the day I listen to mamma talking; at dinner I listen to papa talking; and when papa stops for breath I listen to Johnny talking.

LORD SUMMERHAYS. You make me feel very guilty. I talk too, I'm afraid.

HYPATIA. Oh, I dont mind that, because your talk is a novelty. But it must have been dreadful for your daughters.

LORD SUMMERHAYS. I suppose so.

HYPATIA. If parents would only realize how they bore their children! Three or four times in the last half hour Ive been on the point of screaming.

LORD SUMMERHAYS. Were we very dull?

HYPATIA. Not at all: you were very clever. Thats whats so hard to bear, because it makes it so difficult to avoid listening. You see, I'm young; and I do so want something to happen. My mother tells me that when I'm her age, I shall be only too glad that nothing's happened; but I'm not her age; so what good is that to me? Theres my father in the garden, meditating on his destiny. All very well for him: he's had a destiny to meditate on; but I havnt had any destiny yet. Everything's happened to him: nothing's happened to me. Thats why this unending talk is so maddeningly uninteresting to me.

LORD SUMMERHAYS. It would be worse if we sat in silence.

HYPATIA. No it wouldnt. If you all sat in silence, as if you were waiting for something to happen, then there would be hope even if nothing did happen. But this eternal cackle, cackle, cackle about things in general is only fit for old, old, OLD people. I suppose it means something to them: theyve had their fling. All I listen for is some sign of it ending in something; but just when it seems to be coming to a point, Johnny or papa just starts another hare; and it all begins over again; and I realize that it's never going to lead anywhere and never going to stop. Thats when I want to scream. I wonder how you can stand it.

LORD SUMMERHAYS. Well, I'm old and garrulous myself, you see. Besides, I'm not here of my own free will, exactly. I came because you ordered me to come.

HYPATIA. Didnt you want to come?

LORD SUMMERHAYS. My dear: after thirty years of managing other people's business, men lost the habit of considering what they want or dont want.

HYPATIA. Oh, dont begin to talk about what men do, and about thirty years experience. If you cant get off that subject, youd better send for Johnny and papa and begin it all over again.

LORD SUMMERHAYS. I'm sorry. I beg your pardon.

HYPATIA. I asked you, didnt you want to come?

LORD SUMMERHAYS. I did not stop to consider whether I wanted or not, because when I read your letter I knew I had to come.

HYPATIA. Why?

LORD SUMMERHAYS. Oh come, Miss Tarleton! Really! Really! Dont force me to call you a blackmailer to your face. You have me in your power; and I do what you tell me very obediently. Dont ask me to pretend I do it of my own free will.

HYPATIA. I dont know what a blackmailer is. I havnt even that much experience.

LORD SUMMERHAYS. A blackmailer, my dear young lady, is a person who knows a disgraceful secret in the life of another person, and extorts money from that other person by threatening to make his secret public unless the money is paid.

HYPATIA. I havnt asked you for money.

LORD SUMMERHAYS. No; but you asked me to come down here and talk to you; and you mentioned casually that if I didnt youd have nobody to talk about me to but Bentley. That was a threat, was it not?

HYPATIA. Well, I wanted you to come.

LORD SUMMERHAYS. In spite of my age and my unfortunate talkativeness?

HYPATIA. I like talking to you. I can let myself go with you. I can say things to you I cant say to other people.

LORD SUMMERHAYS. I wonder why?

HYPATIA. Well, you are the only really clever, grown-up, high-class, experienced man I know who has given himself away to me by making an utter fool of himself with me. You cant wrap yourself up in your toga after that. You cant give yourself airs with me.

LORD SUMMERHAYS. You mean you can tell Bentley about me if I do.

HYPATIA. Even if there wasnt any Bentley: even if you didnt care (and I really dont see why you should care so much) still, we never could be on conventional terms with one another again. Besides, Ive got a feeling for you: almost a ghastly sort of love for you.

LORD SUMMERHAYS. (*shrinking*) I beg you—no, please.

HYPATIA. Oh, it's nothing at all flattering; and, of course, nothing wrong, as I suppose youd call it.

LORD SUMMERHAYS. Please believe that I know that. When men of my age—

HYPATIA. (*impatiently*) Oh, do talk about yourself when you mean yourself, and not about men of your age.

LORD SUMMERHAYS. I'll put it as bluntly as I can. When, as you say, I made an utter fool of myself, believe me, I made a poetic fool of myself. I was seduced, not by appetites which, thank Heaven, Ive long outlived: not even by the desire of second childhood for a child companion, but by the innocent impulse to place the delicacy and wisdom and spirituality of my age at the affectionate service of your youth for a few years, at the

end of which you would be a grown, strong, formed—
widow. Alas, my dear, the delicacy of age reckoned, as
usual, without the derision and cruelty of youth. You told
me that you didnt want to be an old man's nurse, and
that you didnt want to have undersized children like
Bentley. It served me right: I dont reproach you: I was
an old fool. But how you can imagine, after that, that I
can suspect you of the smallest feeling for me except the
inevitable feeling of early youth for late age, or imagine
that I have any feeling for you except one of shrinking
humiliation, I cant understand.

HYPATIA. I dont blame you for falling in love with me.
I shall be grateful to you all my life for it, because that
was the first time that anything really interesting happened to me.

LORD SUMMERHAYS. Do you mean to tell me that
nothing of that kind had ever happened before? that no
man had ever—

HYPATIA. Oh, lots. Thats part of the routine of life
here: the very dullest part of it. The young man who
comes a-courting is as familiar an incident in my life as
coffee for breakfast. Of course, he's too much of a gentleman to misbehave himself; and I'm too much of a lady
to let him; and he's shy and sheepish; and I'm correct
and self-possessed; and at last, when I can bear it no
longer, I either frighten him off or give him a chance of
proposing, just to see how he'll do it, and refuse him
because he does it in the same silly way as all the rest.
You dont call that an event in one's life, do you? With
you it was different. I should as soon have expected the
North Pole to fall in love with me as you. You know I'm
only a linendraper's daughter when all's said. I was afraid
of you: you, a great man! a lord! and older than my
father. And then, what a situation it was! Just think of
it! I was engaged to your son; and you knew nothing
about it. He was afraid to tell you: he brought you down
here because he thought if he could throw us together I
could get round you because I was such a ripping girl.

We arranged it all: he and I. We got Papa and Mamma and Johnny out of the way splendidly; and then Bentley took himself off, and left us—you and me!—to take a walk through the heather and admire the scenery of Hindhead. You never dreamt that it was all a plan: that what made me so nice was the way I was playing up to my destiny as the sweet girl that was to make your boy happy. And then! and then! (*She rises to dance and clap her hands in her glee*).

LORD SUMMERHAYS. (*shuddering*) Stop, stop. Can no woman understand a man's delicacy?

HYPATIA. (*revelling in the recollection*) And then—ha, ha!—y o u proposed. You! A father! For your son's girl!

LORD SUMMERHAYS. Stop, I tell you. Dont profane what you dont understand.

HYPATIA. That was something happening at last with a vengeance. It was splendid. It was my first peep behind the scenes. If I'd been seventeen I should have fallen in love with you. Even as it is, I feel quite differently towards you from what I do towards other old men. So (*Offering her hand*) you may kiss my hand if that will be any fun for you.

LORD SUMMERHAYS. (*rising and recoiling to the table, deepiy revolted*) No, no, no. How dare you? (*She laughs mischievously*) How callous youth is! How coarse! How cynical! How ruthlessly cruel!

HYPATIA. Stuff! It's only that youre tired of a great many things Ive never tried.

LORD SUMMERHAYS. It's not alone that. Ive not forgotten the brutality of my own boyhood. But do try to learn, glorious young beast that you are, that age is squeamish, sentimental, fastidious. If you cant understand my holier feelings, at least you know the bodily infirmities of the old. You know that I darent eat all the rich things you gobble up at every meal; that I can't bear the noise and racket and clatter that affect you no more than they affect a stone. Well, my soul is like that too. Spare it: be gentle with it (*He involuntarily puts out his hands to plead: she takes them with a laugh*) If you could possibly think of me as half an angel and half an invalid, we should get on much better together.

HYPATIA. We get on very well, I think. Nobody else ever called me a glorious young beast. I like that. Glorious young beast expresses exactly what I like to be.

LORD SUMMERHAYS. (*extricating his hands and sitting down*) Where on earth did you get these morbid tastes? You seem to have been well brought up in a normal, healthy, respectable, middle-class family. Yet you go on like the most unwholesome product of the rankest Bohemianism.

HYPATIA. Thats just it. I'm fed up with—

LORD SUMMERHAYS. Horrible expression. Dont.

HYPATIA. Oh, I daresay it's vulgar; but theres no other word for it. I'm fed up with nice things: with respectability, with propriety! When a woman has nothing to do, money and respectability mean that nothing is ever allowed to happen to her. I don't want to be good; and I don't want to be bad: I just dont want to be bothered about either good or bad: I want to be an active verb.

LORD SUMMERHAYS. An active verb? Oh, I see. An active verb signifies to be, to do, or to suffer.

HYPATIA. Just so: how clever of you! I want to be; I want to do; and I'm game to suffer if it costs that. But stick here doing nothing but being good and nice and ladylike I simply w o n t. Stay down here with us for a week; and I'll shew you what it means: shew it to you going on day after day, year after year, lifetime after lifetime.

LORD SUMMERHAYS. Shew me what?

HYPATIA. Girls withering into ladies. Ladies withering into old maids. Nursing old women. Running errands for old men. Good for nothing else at last. Oh, you cant imagine the fiendish selfishness of the old people and the maudlin sacrifice of the young. It's more unbearable than any poverty: more horrible than any regular-right-down wickedness. Oh, home! home! parents! family! duty! how I loathe them! How I'd like to see them all blown to bits! The poor escape. The wicked escape. Well, I cant be poor: we're rolling in money: it's no use pretending we're not. But I can be wicked; and I'm quite prepared to be.

LORD SUMMERHAYS. You think that easy?

HYPATIA. Well, isnt it? Being a man, you ought to know.

LORD SUMMERHAYS. It requires some natural talent, which can no doubt be cultivated. It's not really easy to be anything out of the common.

HYPATIA. Anyhow, I mean to make a fight for living.

LORD SUMMERHAYS. Living your own life, I believe the Suffragist phrase is.

HYPATIA. Living a n y life. Living, instead of withering without even a gardener to snip you off when youre rotten.

LORD SUMMERHAYS. Ive lived an active life; but Ive withered all the same.

HYPATIA. No: youve worn out: thats quite different. And youve some life in you yet or you wouldnt have fallen in love with me. You can never imagine how delighted I was to find that instead of being the correct sort of big panjandrum you were supposed to be, you were really an old rip like papa.

LORD SUMMERHAYS. No, no: not about your father: I really cant bear it. And if you must say these terrible things: these heart-wounding shameful things, at least find something prettier to call me than an old rip.

HYPATIA. Well, what w o u l d you call a man proposing to a girl who might be—

LORD SUMMERHAYS. His daughter: yes, I know.

HYPATIA. I was going to say his granddaughter.

LORD SUMMERHAYS. You always have one more blow to get in.

HYPATIA. Youre too sensitive. Did you ever make mud pies when you were a kid—beg pardon: a child.

LORD SUMMERHAYS. I hope not.

HYPATIA. It's a dirty job; but Johnny and I were vulgar enough to like it. I like young people because theyre not too afraid of dirt to live. Ive grown out of the mud pies; but I like slang; and I like bustling you up by saying things that shock you; and I'd rather put up with swearing and smoking than with dull respectability; and there are lots of things that would just shrivel you up that I think rather jolly. Now!

LORD SUMMERHAYS. Ive not the slightest doubt of it. Don't insist.

HYPATIA. It's not your ideal, is it?

LORD SUMMERHAYS. No.

HYPATIA. Shall I tell you why? Your ideal is an old woman. I daresay she's got a young face; but she's an old woman. Old, old, old. Squeamish. Cant stand up to things. Cant enjoy things: not real things. Always on the shrink.

LORD SUMMERHAYS. On the shrink! Detestable expression.

HYPATIA. Bah! you cant stand even a little thing like that. What good are you? Oh, what good are you?

LORD SUMMERHAYS. Dont ask me. I dont know. I dont know. (TARLETON *returns from the vestibule.* HYPATIA *sits down demurely*).

HYPATIA. Well, papa: have you meditated on your destiny?

TARLETON. (*puzzled*) What? Oh! my destiny. Gad, I forgot all about it: Jock started a rabbit and put it clean out of my head. Besides, why should I give way to morbid introspection? Its a sign of madness. Read Lombroso. (*To* LORD SUMMERHAYS) Well, Summerhays, has my little girl been entertaining you?

LORD SUMMERHAYS. Yes. She is a wonderful entertainer.

TARLETON. I think my idea of bringing up a young girl has been rather a success. Dont you listen to this, Patsy: it might make you conceited. She's never been treated like a child. I always said the same thing to her mother. Let her read what she likes. Let her do what she likes. Let her go where she likes. Eh, Patsy?

HYPATIA. Oh yes, if there had only been anything for me to do, any place for me to go, anything I wanted to read.

TARLETON. There, you see! She's not satisfied. Restless. Wants things to happen. Wants adventures to drop out of the sky.

HYPATIA. (*gathering up her work*) If youre going to talk about me and my education, I'm off.

TARLETON. Well, well, off with you. (*To* LORD SUMMERHAYS) She's active, like me. She actually wanted me to put her into the shop.

HYPATIA. Well, they tell me that the girls there have adventures sometimes. (*She goes out through the inner door*).

TARLETON. She had me there, though she doesnt know it, poor innocent lamb! Public scandal exaggerates enormously, of course; but moralize as you will, superabundant vitality is a physical fact that cant be talked away. (*He sits down between the writing table and the sideboard*) Difficult question this, of bringing up children. Between ourselves, it has beaten me. I never was so surprised in my life as when I came to know Johnny as a man of business and found out what he was really like. How did you manage with your sons?

LORD SUMMERHAYS. Well, I really hadnt time to be a father: thats the plain truth of the matter. Their poor dear mother did the usual thing while they were with us. Then of course Eton, Oxford, the usual routine of their class. I saw very little of them, and thought very little about them: how could I? with a whole province on my hands. They and I are—acquaintances. Not, perhaps, quite ordinary acquaintances: theres a sort of—er—I should almost call it a sort of remorse about the way we shake hands (when we do shake hands) which means, I suppose, that we're sorry we dont care more for one another; and I'm afraid we dont meet oftener than we can help. We put each other too much out of countenance. It's really a very difficult relation. To my mind not altogether a natural one.

TARLETON. (*impressed, as usual*) Thats an idea, certainly. I dont think anybody has ever written about that.

LORD SUMMERHAYS. Bentley is the only one who was really my son in any serious sense. He was completely spoilt. When he was sent to a preparatory school he simply yelled until he was sent home. Eton was out of the question; but we managed to tutor him into Oxford. No use: he was sent down. By that time my work was over; and I saw a good deal of him. But I could do nothing with him—except look on. I should have thought your case was quite different. You keep up the middle-class tradition: the day school and the business training instead of the university. I believe in the day school part of it. At all events, you know your own children.

TARLETON. Do we? I'm not so sure of it. Fact is, my dear Summerhays, once childhood is over, once the little animal has got past the stage at which it acquires what you might call a sense of decency, it's all up with the relation between parent and child. You cant get over the fearful shyness of it.

LORD SUMMERHAYS. Shyness?

TARLETON. Yes, shyness. Read Dickens.

LORD SUMMERHAYS. (*surprised*) Dickens!! Of all authors, Charles Dickens! Are you serious?

TARLETON. I dont mean his books. Read his letters to his family. Read any man's letters to his children. Theyre not human. Theyre not about himself or themselves. Theyre about hotels, scenery, about the weather, about getting wet and losing the train and what he saw on the road and all that. Not a word about himself. Forced. Shy. Duty letters. All fit to be published: that says everything. I tell you theres a wall ten feet thick and ten miles high between parent and child. I know what I'm talking about. Ive girls in my employment: girls and young men. I had ideas on the subject. I used to go to the parents and tell

them not to let their children go out into the world without instruction in the dangers and temptations they were
going to be thrown into. What did every one of the
mothers say to me? "Oh, sir, how could I speak of such
things to my own daughter?" The men said I was quite
right; but they didnt do it, any more than I'd been able
to do it myself to Johnny. I had to leave books in his
way; and I felt just awful when I did it. Believe me,
Summerhays, the relation between the young and the old
should be an innocent relation. It should be something
they could talk about. Well, the relation between parent
and child may be an affectionate relation. It may be a
useful relation. It may be a necessary relation. But it can
never be an innocent relation. Youd die rather than allude
to it. Depend on it, in a thousand years itll be considered
bad form to know who your father and mother are. Em-
barrassing. Better hand Bentley over to me. I can look
him in the face and talk to him as man to man. You can
have Johnny.

LORD SUMMERHAYS. Thank you. Ive lived so long in a
country where a man may have fifty sons, who are no
more to him than a regiment of soldiers, that I'm afraid
Ive lost the English feeling about it.

TARLETON. (*restless again*) You mean Jinghiskahn.
Ah yes. Good thing the empire. Educates us. Opens our
minds. Knocks the Bible out of us. And civilizes the other
chaps.

LORD SUMMERHAYS. Yes: it civilizes t h e m. And it
uncivilizes us. Their gain. Our loss. Tarleton, believe me,
our loss.

TARLETON. Well, why not? Averages out the human
race. Makes the nigger half an Englishman. Makes the
Englishman half a nigger.

LORD SUMMERHAYS. Speaking as the unfortunate
Englishman in question, I dont like the process. If I had
my life to live over again, I'd stay at home and super-
civilize myself.

TARLETON. Nonsense! don't be selfish. Think how

youve improved the other chaps. Look at the Spanish empire! Bad job for Spain, but splendid for South America. Look at what the Romans did for Britain! They burst up and had to clear out; but think of all they taught us? They were the making of us: I believe there was a Roman camp on Hindhead: I'll shew it to you tomorrow. Thats the good side of Imperialism: it's unselfish. I despise the Little Englanders: theyre always thinking about England. Small-minded. I'm for the Parliament of man, the federation of the world. Read Tennyson. (*He settles down again.*) Then theres the great food question.

LORD SUMMERHAYS. (*apprehensively*) Need we go into that this afternoon?

TARLETON. No; but I wish youd tell the Chickabiddy that the Jinghiskahns eat no end of toasted cheese, and that it's the secret of their amazing health and long life!

LORD SUMMERHAYS. Unfortunately they are neither healthy nor long lived. And they dont eat toasted cheese.

TARLETON. There you are! They would be if they ate it. Anyhow, say what you like, provided the moral is a Welsh rabbit for my supper.

LORD SUMMERHAYS. British morality in a nutshell!

TARLETON. (*hugely amused*) Yes, Ha ha! Awful hypocrites, aint we?

They are interrupted by excited cries from the grounds.

HYPATIA. ⎞ Papa! Mamma! Come out as fast as you
⎟ can. Quick. Quick.
BENTLEY. ⎠ Hello, governor! Come out. An aeroplane. Look, look.

TARLETON. (*starting up*) Aeroplane! Did he say an aeroplane?

LORD SUMMERHAYS. Aeroplane! (*A shadow falls on the pavilion; and some of the glass at the top is shattered and falls on the floor.* TARLETON *and* LORD SUMMERHAYS *rush out through the pavilion into the garden*).

HYPATIA.	Take care. Take care of the chimney.
BENTLEY.	Come this side; it's coming right where youre standing.
TARLETON.	Hallo! where the devil are you coming? youll have my roof off.
LORD SUMMERHAYS.	He's lost control.

MRS TARLETON. Look, look, Hypatia. There are two people in it.

BENTLEY. Theyve cleared it. Well steered!

TARLETON.	Yes; but theyre coming slam into the greenhouse.
LORD SUMMERHAYS.	Look out for the glass.
MRS TARLETON.	Theyll break all the glass. Theyll spoil all the grapes.
BENTLEY.	Mind where youre coming. He'll save it. No: theyre down.

An appalling crash of breaking glass is heard. Everybody shrieks.

MRS TARLETON.	Oh, are they killed? John: are they killed?
LORD SUMMERHAYS.	Are you hurt? Is anything broken? Can you stand?
HYPATIA.	Oh, you must be hurt. Are you sure? Shall I get you some water? Or some wine?
TARLETON.	Are you all right? Sure you wont have some brandy just to take off the shock.

THE AVIATOR. No, thank you. Quite right. Not a scratch. I assure you I'm all right.

BENTLEY. What luck! And what a smash! You a r e a lucky chap, I can tell you.

The AVIATOR *and* TARLETON *come in through the pavilion, followed by* LORD SUMMERHAYS *and* BENTLEY, *the* AVIATOR *on* TARLETON'S *right.* BENTLEY *passes the* AVIATOR *and turns to have an admiring look at him.* LORD SUMMERHAYS *overtakes* TARLETON *less pointedly on the opposite side with the same object.*

THE AVIATOR. I'm really very sorry. I'm afraid Ive knocked your vinery into a cocked hat. (*Effusively*) You don't mind, do you?

TARLETON. Not a bit. Come in and have some tea. Stay to dinner. Stay over the week-end All my life Ive wanted to fly.

THE AVIATOR. (*taking off his goggles*) Youre really more than kind.

BENTLEY. Why, it's Joey Percival.

PERCIVAL. Hallo, Ben! That you?

TARLETON. What! The man with three fathers!

PERCIVAL. Oh! has Ben been talking about me?

TARLETON. Consider yourself as one of the family— if you will do me the honor. And your friend too. Wheres your friend?

PERCIVAL. Oh, by the way! before he comes in: let me explain. I dont know him.

TARLETON. Eh?

PERCIVAL. Havnt even looked at him. I'm trying to make a club record with a passenger. The club supplied the passenger. He just got in; and Ive been too busy handling the aeroplane to look at him. I havnt said a word to him; and I cant answer for him socially; but he's an ideal passenger for a flyer. He saved me from a smash.

LORD SUMMERHAYS. I saw it. It was extraordinary. When you were thrown out he held on to the top bar with one hand. You came past him in the air, going straight for the glass. He caught you and turned you off into the flower bed, and then lighted beside you like a bird.

PERCIVAL. How he kept his head I cant imagine. Frankly, *I* didnt.

The PASSENGER, *also begoggled, comes in through the pavilion with* JOHNNY *and the two ladies. The* PASSENGER *comes between* PERCIVAL *and* TARLETON, MRS TARLETON *between* LORD SUMMERHAYS *and her husband,* HYPATIA *between* PERCIVAL *and* BENTLEY, *and* JOHNNY *to* BENTLEY'S *right.*

TARLETON. Just discussing your prowess, my dear sir. Magnificent. Youll stay to dinner. Youll stay the night. Stay over the week. The Chickabiddy will be delighted.

MRS TARLETON. Wont you take off your goggles and have some tea? (*The* PASSENGER *begins to remove the goggles*).

TARLETON. Do. Have a wash. Johnny: take the gentleman to your room: I'll look after Mr. Percival. They must—

By this time the PASSENGER *has got the goggles off, and stands revealed as a remarkably good-looking woman.*

MRS TARLETON. Well I never!!! ⎫
BENTLEY. (*in a whisper*) Oh, I say! ⎪
JOHNNY. By George! ⎪
LORD SUMMERHAYS. A lady! ⎬ (*All*
HYPATIA. A woman! ⎪ *together*)
TARLETON. (*to* PERCIVAL) You never ⎪
told me— ⎪
PERCIVAL. I hadnt the least idea— ⎭

An embarrassed pause.

PERCIVAL. I assure you if I'd had the faintest notion that my passenger was a lady I shouldnt have left you to shift for yourself in that selfish way.

LORD SUMMERHAYS. The lady seems to have shifted for both very effectually, sir.

PERCIVAL. Saved my life. I admit it most gratefully.

TARLETON. I must apologize, madam, for having offered you the civilities appropriate to the opposite sex. And yet, why opposite? We are all human: males and females of the same species. When the dress is the same the distinction vanishes. I'm proud to receive in my house a lady of evident refinement and distinction. Allow me to introduce myself: Tarleton: John Tarleton (*Seeing conjecture in the passenger's eye*) yes, yes: Tarleton's Underwear. My wife, Mrs Tarleton: youll excuse me for having in what I had taken to be a confidence between man and man alluded to her as the Chickabiddy. My daughter Hypatia, who has always wanted some adventure to drop out of the sky, and is now, I hope, satisfied at last. Lord Summerhays: a man known wherever the British flag waves. His son Bentley, engaged to Hypatia. Mr Joseph Percival, the promising son of three highly intellectual fathers.

HYPATIA. (*startled*) Bentley's friend? (BENTLEY *nods*).

TARLETON. (*continuing, to the passenger*) May I now ask to be allowed the pleasure of knowing your name?

THE PASSENGER. My name is Lina Szczepanowska. (*Pronouncing it Sh-Chepanovska*).

PERCIVAL. Sh—I beg your pardon?

LINA. Szczepanowska.

PERCIVAL. (*dubiously*) Thank you.

TARLETON. (*very politely*) Would you mind saying it again?

LINA. Say fish.

TARLETON. Fish.

LINA. Say church.

TARLETON. Church.

LINA. Say fish church.

TARLETON. (*remonstrating*) But it's not good sense.

LINA. (*inexorable*) Say fish church.

TARLETON. Fish church.

LINA. Again.

TARLETON. No, but— (*Resigning himself*) fish church.

LINA. Now say Szczepanowska.

TARLETON. Szczepanowska. Got it, by Gad. (*A sibilant whispering becomes audible: they are all saying Sh-ch to themselves*) Szczepanowska! Not an English name, is it?

LINA. Polish. I'm a Pole.

TARLETON. (*dithyrambically*) Ah yes. What other nation, madame, could have produced your magical personality? Your countrywomen have always appealed to our imagination. Women of Destiny! beautiful! musical! passionate! tragic! You will be at home here: my own temperament is pre-eminently Polish. Wont you sit down? *The group breaks up.* JOHNNY *and* BENTLEY *hurry to the pavilion and fetch the two wicker chairs.* JOHNNY *gives his to* LINA. HYPATIA *and* PERCIVAL *take the chairs at the worktable.* LORD SUMMERHAYS *gives the chair at the vestibule end of the writing table to* MRS TARLETON; *and* BENTLEY *replaces it with a wicker chair, which* LORD SUMMERHAYS *takes.* JOHNNY *remains standing behind the worktable,* BENTLEY *behind his father.*

MRS TARLETON. (*to* LINA) Have some tea now, wont you?

LINA. I never drink tea.

TARLETON. (*sitting down at the end of the writing table nearest* LINA) Bad thing to aeroplane on, I should imagine. Too jumpy. Been up much?

LINA. Not in an aeroplane. Ive parachuted; but thats child's play.

MRS TARLETON. But arnt you very foolish to run such a dreadful risk?

LINA. You cant live without running risks.

MRS TARLETON. Oh, what a thing to say! Didnt you know you might have been killed?

LINA. That was why I went up.

HYPATIA. Of course. Cant you understand the fascination of the thing? the novelty! the daring! the sense of something happening!

LINA. Oh no. It's too tame a business for that. I went up for family reasons.

TARLETON. Eh? What? Family reasons?

MRS TARLETON. I hope it wasnt to spite your mother?

PERCIVAL. (*quickly*) Or your husband?

LINA. I'm not married. And why should I want to spite my mother?

HYPATIA. (*aside to* PERCIVAL) That was clever of you, Mr Percival.

PERCIVAL. What?

HYPATIA. To find out.

TARLETON. I'm in a difficulty. I cant understand a lady going up in an aeroplane for family reasons. It's rude to be curious and ask questions; but then it's inhuman to be indifferent, as if you didnt care.

LINA. I'll tell you with pleasure. For the last hundred and fifty years, not a single day has passed without some member of my family risking his life—or her life. It's a point of honor with us to keep up that tradition. Usually several of us do it; but it happens that just at this moment it is being kept up by one of my brothers only. Early this morning I got a telegram from him to say that there had been a fire, and that he could do nothing for the rest of the week. Fortunately I had an invitation from the Aerial League to see this gentleman try to break the passenger record. I appealed to the President of the League to let me save the honor my family. He arranged it for me.

TARLETON. Oh, I must be dreaming. This is stark raving nonsense.

LINA. (*quietly*) You are quite awake, sir.

JOHNNY. We cant all be dreaming the same thing, governor.

TARLETON. Of course not, you duffer; but then I'm dreaming y o u as well as the lady.

MRS TARLETON. Don't be silly, John. The lady is only joking, I'm sure. (*To* LINA) I suppose your luggage is in the aeroplane.

PERCIVAL. Luggage was out of the question. If I stay to dinner I'm afraid I cant change unless youll lend me some clothes.

MRS TARLETON. Do you mean n e i t h e r of you?

PERCIVAL. I'm afraid so.

MRS TARLETON. Oh well, never mind: Hypatia will lend the lady a gown.

LINA. Thank you: I'm quite comfortable as I am. I am not accustomed to gowns: they hamper me and make me feel ridiculous; so if you dont mind I shall not change.

MRS TARLETON. Well, I'm beginning to think I'm doing a bit of dreaming myself.

HYPATIA. (*impatiently*) Oh, it's all right, mamma. Johnny: look after Mr Percival. (*To* LINA, *rising*) Come with me. (LINA *follows her to the inner door. They all rise*).

JOHNNY. (*to* PERCIVAL) I'll shew you.

PERCIVAL. Thank you. (LINA *goes out with* HYPATIA, *and* PERCIVAL *with* JOHNNY).

MRS TARLETON. Well, this is a nice thing to happen! And look at the greenhouse! Itll cost thirty pounds to mend it. People have no right to do such things. And you invited them to dinner too! What sort of woman is that to have in our house when you know that all Hindhead will be calling on us to see that aeroplane? Bunny: come with me and help me to get all the people out of the grounds: I declare they came running as if theyd sprung up out of the earth. (*She makes for the inner door*).

TARLETON. No: dont you trouble, Chickabiddy: I'll tackle em.

MRS TARLETON. Indeed youll do nothing of the kind: youll stay here quietly with Lord Summerhays. Youd invite them all to dinner. Come, Bunny. (*She goes out, followed by* BENTLEY. LORD SUMMERHAYS *sits down again*).

TARLETON. Singularly beautiful woman, Summerhays. What do you make of her? She must be a princess. Whats this family of warriors and statesmen that risk their lives every day?

LORD SUMMERHAYS. They are evidently not warriors and statesmen, or they wouldnt do that.

TARLETON. Well, then, what the devil a r e they?

LORD SUMMERHAYS. I think I know. The last time I saw that lady, she did something I should not have thought possible.

TARLETON. What was that?

LORD SUMMERHAYS. Well, she walked backwards along a taut wire without a balancing pole and turned a somersault in the middle. I remember that her name was Lina, and that the other name was foreign; though I dont recollect it.

TARLETON. Szcz! You couldnt have forgotten that if youd heard it.

LORD SUMMERHAYS. I didnt hear it: I only saw it on a program. But it's clear she's an acrobat. It explains how she saved Percival. And it accounts for her family pride.

TARLETON. An acrobat, eh? Good! good! good! Summerhays: that brings her within reach. Thats better than a princess. I steeled this evergreen heart of mine when I thought she was a princess. Now I shall let it be touched. She is accessible. Good.

LORD SUMMERHAYS. I hope you are not serious. Remember: you have a family. You have a position. You are not in your first youth.

TARLETON. No matter.

Theres magic in the night.
When the heart is young.

My heart is young. Besides, I'm a married man, not a widower like you. A married man can do anything he likes if his wife dont mind. A widower cant be too careful.

Not that I would have you think me an unprincipled man or a bad husband. I'm not. But Ive a superabundance of vitality. Read Pepys' Diary.

LORD SUMMERHAYS. The woman is your guest, Tarleton.

TARLETON. Well, is she? A woman I bring into my house is my guest. A woman y o u bring into my house is my guest. But a woman who drops bang down out of the sky into my greenhouse and smashes every blessed pane of glass in it must take her chance.

LORD SUMMERHAYS. Still, you know that my name must not be associated with any scandal. Youll be careful, wont you?

TARLETON. Oh Lord, yes! Yes, yes, yes, yes, yes. I was only joking, of course. (MRS TARLETON *comes back through the inner door*).

MRS TARLETON. Well I never! John: I dont think that young woman's right in her head. Do you know what she's just asked for?

TARLETON. Champagne?

MRS TARLETON. No. She wants a Bible and six oranges.

TARLETON. What?

MRS TARLETON. A Bible and six oranges.

TARLETON. I understand the oranges: she's doing an orange cure of some sort. But what on earth does she want the Bible for?

MRS TARLETON. I'm sure I cant imagine. She cant be right in her head.

LORD SUMMERHAYS. Perhaps she wants to read it.

MRS TARLETON. But why should she? on a weekday at all events. What would you advise me to do, Lord Summerhays?

LORD SUMMERHAYS. Well, is there a Bible in the house?

TARLETON. Stacks of em. Theres the family Bible, and the Doré Bible, and the parallel revised version Bible, and the Doves Press Bible, and Johnny's Bible and Bobby's Bible and Patsy's Bible and the Chickabiddy's Bible and my Bible;and I daresay the servants could raise a few more between them. Let her have the lot.

MRS TARLETON. Dont talk like that before Lord Summerhays, John.

LORD SUMMERHAYS. It doesnt matter, Mrs Tarleton: in Jinghiskahn it was a punishable offence to expose a Bible for sale. The empire has no religion. (LINA *comes in. She has left her cap in* HYPATIA'S *room, but has made no other change. She stops just inside the door, holding it open, evidently not intending to stay*).

LINA. Oh, Mrs Tarleton, shall I be making myself very troublesome if I ask for a music-stand in my room as well?

TARLETON. Not at all. You can have the piano if you like. Or the gramophone. Have the gramophone?

LINA. No, thank you: no music.

MRS TARLETON. (*going towards her*) Do you think it's good for you to eat so many oranges? Arnt you afraid of getting jaundice?

LINA. Not in the least. But billiard balls will do quite as well.

MRS TARLETON But you cant eat billiard balls, child!

TARLETON. Get em, Chickabiddy. I understand. (*He imitates a juggler tossing up balls*) Eh?

LINA. (*going to him, past his wife*) Just so.

TARLETON. Billiard balls and cues? Plates, knives, and forks? Two paraffin lamps and a hatstand?

LINA. No: that is popular low-class business. In our family we touch nothing but classical work. Anybody can do lamps and hatstands. *I* can do silver bullets. That is really hard. (*She passes on to* LORD SUMMERHAYS, *and looks gravely down at him as he sits by the writing table*).

MRS TARLETON. Well, I'm sure I dont know what youre talking about; and I only hope you know yourselves. However, you shall have what you want, of course. (*She goes out through the inner door*).

LORD SUMMERHAYS. Will you forgive my curiosity? What is the Bible for?

LINA. To quiet my soul.

LORD SUMMERHAYS. (*with a sigh*) Ah yes, yes. It no longer quiets mine, I am sorry to say.

LINA. That is because you do not know how to read it. Put it up before you on a stand; and open it at the Psalms. When you can read them and understand them, quite quietly and happily, and keep six balls in the air all the time, you are in perfect condition; and youll never make a mistake that evening. If you find you cant do that, then go and pray until you can. And be very careful t h a t evening.

LORD SUMMERHAYS. Is that the usual form of test in your profession?

LINA. Nothing that we Szczepanowskis do is usual, my lord.

LORD SUMMERHAYS. Are you all so wonderful?

LINA. It is our profession to be wonderful.

LORD SUMMERHAYS. Do you never condescend to do as common people do? For instance, do you not pray as common people pray?

LINA. Common people do not pray, my lord: they only beg.

LORD SUMMERHAYS. You never ask for anything?

LINA. No.

LORD SUMMERHAYS. Then why do you pray?

LINA. To remind myself that I have a soul.

TARLETON. (*walking about*) True. Fine. Good. Beautiful. All this damned materialism: what good is it to anybody? Ive got a soul: dont tell me I havnt. Cut me up and you cant find it. Cut up a steam engine and you cant find the steam. But, by George, it makes the engine go. Say what you will, Summerhays, the divine spark is a fact.

LORD SUMMERHAYS. Have I denied it?

TARLETON. Our whole civilization is a denial of it. Read Walt Whitman.

LORD SUMMERHAYS. I shall go to the billiard room and get the balls for you.

LINA. Thank you. (LORD SUMMERHAYS *goes out through the vestibule door*).

TARLETON. (*going to her*) Listen to me. (*She turns quickly*) What you said just now was beautiful. You touch chords. You appeal to the poetry in a man. You inspire him. Come now! Youre a woman of the world: youre independent: you must have driven lots of men crazy. You know the sort of man I am, dont you? See through me at a glance eh?

LINA. Yes. (*She sits down quietly in the chair* LORD SUMMERHAYS *has just left*).

TARLETON. Good. Well, do you like me? Dont misunderstand me: I'm perfectly aware that youre not going to fall in love at first sight with a ridiculous old shopkeeper. I cant help that ridiculous old shopkeeper. I have to carry him about with me whether I like it or not. I have to pay for his clothes, though I hate the cut of them: especially the waistcoat. I have to look at him in the glass while I'm shaving. I loathe him because he's a living lie. My soul's not like that: it's like yours. I want to make a fool of myself. About you. Will you let me?

LINA. (*very calm*) How much will you pay?

TARLETON. Nothing. But I'll throw as many sovereigns as you like into the sea to shew you that I'm in earnest.

LINA. Are those your usual terms?

TARLETON. No. I never made that bid before.

LINA. (*producing a dainty little book and preparing to write in it*) What did you say your name was?

TARLETON. John Tarleton. The great John Tarleton of Tarleton's Underwear.

LINA. (*writing*) T-a-r-l-e-t-o-n. Er—? (*She looks up at him inquiringly*).

TARLETON. (*promptly*). Fifty-eight.

LINA. Thank you. I keep a list of all my offers. I like to know what I'm considered worth.

TARLETON. Let me look.

LINA. (*offering the book to him*) It's in Polish.

TARLETON. Thats no good. Is mine the lowest offer?

LINA. No: the highest.

TARLETON. What do most of them come to? Diamonds? Motor cars? Furs? Villa at Monte Carlo?

LINA. Oh yes: all that. And sometimes the devotion of a lifetime.

TARLETON. Fancy that! A young man offering a woman his old age as a temptation!

LINA. By the way, you did not say how long.

TARLETON. Until you get tired of me.

LINA. Or until you get tired of me?

TARLETON. I never get tired. I never go on long enough for that. But when it becomes so grand, so inspiring that I feel that everything must be an anti-climax after that, then I run away.

LINA. Does she let you go without a struggle?

TARLETON. Yes. Glad to get rid of me. When love takes a man as it takes me—when it makes him great—it frightens a woman.

LINA. The lady here is your wife, isnt she? Dont you care for her?

TARLETON. Yes. And mind! she comes first always. I reserve her dignity even when I sacrifice my own. Youll respect that point of honor, wont you?

LINA. Only a point of honor?

TARLETON. (*impulsively*) No, by God! a point of affection as well.

LINA. (*smiling, pleased with him*). Shake hands, old pal. (*She rises and offers him her hand frankly*).

TARLETON. (*giving his hand rather dolefully*). Thanks. That means no, doesnt it?

LINA. It means something that will last longer than yes. I like you. I admit you to my friendship. What a pity you were not trained when you were young! Youd be young still.

TARLETON. I suppose, to an athlete like you, I'm pretty awful, eh?

LINA. Shocking.

TARLETON. Too much crumb. Wrinkles. Yellow patches

that wont come off. Short wind. I know. I'm ashamed of myself. I could do nothing on the high rope.

LINA. Oh yes: I could put you in a wheelbarrow and run you along, two hundred feet up.

TARLETON. (*shuddering*) Ugh! Well, I'd do even that for you. Read The Master Builder.

LINA. Have you learnt everything from books?

TARLETON. Well, have you learnt everything from the flying trapeze?

LINA. On the flying trapeze there is often another woman; and her life is in your hands every night and your life in hers.

TARLETON. Lina: I'm going to make a fool of myself. I'm going to cry. (*He crumples into the nearest chair*).

LINA. Pray instead: don't cry. Why should you cry? Youre not the first Ive said no to.

TARLETON. If you had said yes, should I have been the first then?

LINA. What right have you to ask? Have I asked am *I* the first?

TARLETON. Youre right: a vulgar question. To a man like me, everybody is the first. Life renews itself.

LINA. The youngest child is the sweetest.

TARLETON. Dont probe too deep, Lina. It hurts.

LINA. You must get out of the habit of thinking that these things matter so much. It's linendraperish.

TARLETON. Youre quite right. Ive often said so. All the same, it d o e s matter; for I want to cry. (*He buries his face in his arms on the worktable and sobs*).

LINA. (*going to him*) O la la! (*She slaps him vigorously, but not unkindly, on the shoulder*) Courage, old pal, courage! Have you a gymnasium here?

TARLETON. Theres a trapeze and bars and things in the billiard room.

LINA. Come. You need a few exercises. I'll teach you how to stop crying. (*She takes his arm and leads him off into the vestibule*).

A young man, cheaply dressed and strange in manner, appears in the garden; steals to the pavilion door; and looks in. Seeing that there is nobody, he enters cautiously until he has come far enough to see into the hatstand corner. He draws a revolver, and examines it, apparently to make sure that it is loaded. Then his attention is caught by the Turkish bath. He looks down the lunette, and opens the panels.

HYPATIA. (*calling in the garden*) Mr Percival! Mr Percival! Where are you? (*The young man makes for the door, but sees* PERCIVAL *coming. He turns and bolts into the Turkish bath, which he closes upon himself just in time to escape being caught by* PERCIVAL, *who runs in through the pavilion, bareheaded. He also, it appears, is in search of a hiding-place; for he stops and turns between the two tables to take a survey of the room; then runs into corner between the end of the sideboard and the wall.* HYPATIA, *excited, mischievous, her eyes glowing, runs in, precisely on his trail; turns at the same spot; and discovers him just as he makes a dash for the pavilion door. She flies back and intercepts him.*) Aha! Arnt you glad Ive caught you?

PERCIVAL. (*illhumoredly turning away from her and coming towards the writing table*) No I'm not. Confound it, what sort of girl are you? What sort of house is this? Must I throw all good manners to the winds?

HYPATIA. (*following him*) Do, do, do, do, do. This is the house of a respectable shopkeeper, enormously rich. This is the respectable shopkeeper's daughter, tired of good manners. (*Slipping her left hand into his right*) Come, handsome young man, and play with the respectable shopkeeper's daughter.

PERCIVAL. (*withdrawing quickly from her touch*) No, no: dont you know you mustnt go on like this with a perfect stranger?

HYPATIA. Dropped down from the sky. Dont you know that you must always go on like this when you get the chance? You must come to the top of the hill and chase me through the bracken. You may kiss me if you catch me.

PERCIVAL. I shall do nothing of the sort.

HYPATIA. Yes, you will: you can't help yourself. Come along. (*She seizes his sleeve*) Fool, fool: come along. Dont you want to?

PERCIVAL. No: certainly not. I should never be forgiven if I did it.

HYPATIA. Youll never forgive yourself if you dont.

PERCIVAL. Nonsense. Youre engaged to Ben. Ben's my friend. What do you take me for?

HYPATIA. Ben's old. Ben was born old. Theyre all old here, except you and me and the man-woman or woman-man or whatever you call her that came with you. They never do anything: they only discuss whether what other people do is right. Come and give them something to discuss.

PERCIVAL. I will do nothing incorrect.

HYPATIA. Oh, dont be afraid, little boy: youll get nothing but a kiss; and I'll fight like the devil to keep you from getting that. But we must play on the hill and race through the heather.

PERCIVAL. Why?

HYPATIA. Because we want to, handsome young man.

PERCIVAL. But if everybody went on in this way—

HYPATIA. How happy! oh how happy the world would be!

PERCIVAL. But the consequences may be serious.

HYPATIA. Nothing is worth doing unless the consequences may be serious. My father says so; and I'm my father's daughter.

PERCIVAL. I'm the son of three fathers. I mistrust these wild impulses.

HYPATIA. Take care. Youre letting the moment slip. I feel the first chill of the wave of prudence. Save me.

PERCIVAL. Really, Miss Tarleton! (*She strikes him across the face*) Damn you! (*Recovering himself, hor-*

rified at his lapse) I beg your pardon; but since weve both forgotten ourselves, youll please allow me to leave the house. (*He turns towards the inner door, having left his cap in the bedroom*).

HYPATIA. (*standing in his way*) Are you ashamed of having said "Damn you" to me?

PERCIVAL. I had no right to say it. I'm very much ashamed of it. I have already begged your pardon.

HYPATIA. And youre not ashamed of having said "Really, Miss Tarleton!"?

PERCIVAL. Why should I?

HYPATIA. O man, man! mean, stupid, cowardly, selfish masculine male man! You ought to have been a governess. I was expelled from school for saying that the very next person that said "Really, Miss Tarleton!" to me, I would strike across the face. You were the next.

PERCIVAL. I had no intention of being offensive. Surely there is nothing that can wound any lady in— (*He hesitates, not quite convinced*) At least—er—I really didnt mean to be disagreeable.

HYPATIA. Liar.

PERCIVAL. Of course if youre going to insult me, I am quite helpless. Youre a woman: you can say what you like.

HYPATIA. And you can only say what you dare. Poor wretch: it isnt much. (*He bites his lip, and sits down, very much annoyed*) Really, Mr Percival! You sit down in the presence of a lady and leave her standing. (*He rises hastily*). Ha ha! Really, Mr Percival! Oh really, really, really, really, really, Mr Percival! How do you like it? Wouldnt you rather I damned you?

PERCIVAL. Miss Tarleton—

HYPATIA. (*caressingly*) Hypatia, Joey. Patsy, if you like.

PERCIVAL. Look here: this is no good. You want to do what you like?

HYPATIA. Dont you!

PERCIVAL. No. Ive been too well brought up. Ive argued

all through this thing; and I tell you I'm not prepared to cast off the social bond. It's like a corset: it's a support to the figure even if it does squeeze and deform it a bit. I want to be free.

HYPATIA. Well, I'm tempting you to be free.

PERCIVAL. Not at all. Freedom, my good girl, means being able to count on how other people will behave. If every man who dislikes me is to throw a handful of mud in my face, and every woman who likes me is to behave like Potiphar's wife, then I shall be a slave: the slave of uncertainty: the slave of fear: the worst of all slaveries. How would you like it if every laborer you met in the road were to make love to you? No. Give me the blessed protection of a good stiff conventionality among thoroughly well-brought-up ladies and gentlemen.

HYPATIA. Another talker! Men like conventions because men made them. I didnt make them: I dont like them: I wont keep them. Now, what will you do?

PERCIVAL. Bolt. (*He runs out through the pavilion*).

HYPATIA. I'll catch you. (*She dashes off in pursuit*).

During this conversation the head of the scandalized man in the Turkish bath has repeatedly risen from the lunette, with a strong expression of moral shock. It vanishes abruptly as the two turn towards it in their flight. At the same moment TARLETON *comes back through the vestibule door, exhausted by severe and unaccustomed exercise.*

TARLETON. (*looking after the flying figures with amazement*) Hallo, Patsy: whats up? Another aeroplane? (*They are far too preoccupied to hear him; and he is left staring after them as they rush away through the garden. He goes to the pavilion door and looks up; but the heavens are empty. His exhaustion disables him from further inquiry. He dabs his brow with his handkerchief, and walks stiffly to the nearest convenient support, which happens to be the Turkish bath. He props himself upon it with his elbow, and covers his eyes with his hand for a moment. After a few sighing breaths, he feels a little better, and uncovers his eyes. The man's head rises from the lunette a few inches from his nose. He recoils from the bath with a violent start*) Oh Lord! My brain's gone. (*Calling piteously*) Chickabiddy! (*He staggers down to the writing table*).

THE MAN. (*coming out of the bath, pistol in hand*) Another sound; and youre a dead man.

TARLETON. (*braced*) Am I! Well, youre a live one: thats one comfort. I thought you were a ghost. (*He sits down, quite undisturbed by the pistol*) Who are you; and what the devil were you doing in my new Turkish bath?

THE MAN. (*with tragic intensity*) I am the son of Lucinda Titmus.

TARLETON. (*the name conveying nothing to him*) Indeed? And how is she? Quite well, I hope, eh?

THE MAN. She is dead. Dead, my God! and you are alive.

TARLETON. (*Unimpressed by the tragedy, but sympathetic*) Oh! Lost your mother? Thats sad. I'm sorry. But we cant all have the luck to die before our mothers, and be nursed out of the world by the hands that nursed us into it.

THE MAN. Much you care, damn you!

TARLETON. Oh, dont cut up rough. Face it like a man. You see I didnt know your mother; but Ive no doubt she was an excellent woman.

THE MAN. Not know her! Do you dare to stand there by her open grave and deny that you knew her?

TARLETON. (*trying to recollect*) What did you say her name was?

THE MAN. Lucinda Titmus.

TARLETON. Well, I ought to remember a rum name like that if I ever heard it. But I dont. Have you a photograph or anything?

THE MAN. Forgotten even the name of your victim!

TARLETON. Oh! she was my victim, was she?

THE MAN. She was. And you shall see her face again before you die, dead as she is. I h a v e a photograph.

TARLETON. Good.

THE MAN. Ive two photographs.

TARLETON. Still better. Treasure the mother's pictures. Good boy!

THE MAN. One of them as you knew her. The other as she became when you flung her aside, and she withered into an old woman.

TARLETON. She'd have done that anyhow, my lad. We all grow old. Look at m e! (*Seeing that the man is embarrassed by his pistol in fumbling for the photographs with his left hand in his breast pocket*) Let me hold the gun for you.

THE MAN. (*retreating to the worktable*) Stand back. Do you take me for a fool?

TARLETON. Well, youre a little upset, naturally. It does you credit.

THE MAN. Look here, upon this picture and on this. (*He holds out the two photographs like a hand at cards, and points to them with the pistol*).

TARLETON. Good. Read Shakespear: he has a word for every occasion. (*He takes the photographs, one in each hand, and looks from one to the other, pleased and interested, but without any sign of recognition*) What a pretty girl! Very pretty. I can imagine myself falling in love with her when I was your age. I wasnt a badlooking young fellow myself in those days. (*Looking at the other*) Curious that we should both have gone the same way.

THE MAN. You and she the same way! What do you mean?

TARLETON. Both got stout, I mean.

THE MAN. Would you have had her deny herself food?

TARLETON. No: it wouldnt have been any use. It's constitutional. No matter how little you eat you put on flesh if youre made that way. (*He resumes his study of the earlier photograph*).

THE MAN. Is that all the feeling that rises in you at the sight of the face you once knew so well?

TARLETON. (*too much absorbed in the portrait to heed him*) Funny that I cant remember! Let this be a lesson to you, young man. I could go into court tomorrow and swear I never saw that face before in my life if it wasnt for that brooch (*Pointing to the photograph*) Have you got that brooch, by the way? (THE MAN *again resorts to his breast pocket*) You seem to carry the whole family property in that pocket.

THE MAN. (*producing a brooch*) Here it is to prove my bona fides.

TARLETON. (*pensively putting the photographs on the table and taking the brooch*) I bought that brooch in Cheapside from a man with a yellow wig and a cast in his left eye. I've never set eyes on him from that day to this. And yet I remember that man; and I cant remember your mother.

THE MAN. Monster! Without conscience! without even memory! You left her to her shame—

TARLETON. (*throwing the brooch on the table and rising pepperily*) Come, come, young man! none of that. Respect the romance of your mother's youth. Dont you start throwing stones at her. I dont recall her features just at this moment; but Ive no doubt she was kind to me and we were happy together. If you have a word to say against her, take yourself out of my house and say it elsewhere.

THE MAN. What sort of a joker are you? Are you trying to put me in the wrong, when you have to answer to me for a crime that would make every honest man spit at you as you passed in the street if I were to make it known?

TARLETON. You read a good deal, dont you?

THE MAN. What if I do? What has that to do with your infamy and my mother's doom?

TARLETON. There, you see! Doom! Thats not good sense; but it's literature. Now it happens that I'm a tremendous reader: always was. When I was your age I read books of that sort by the bushel: the Doom sort, you know. It's odd, isnt it, that you and I should be like one another in that respect? Can you account for it in any way?

THE MAN. No. What are you driving at?

TARLETON. Well, do you know who your father was?

THE MAN. I see what you mean now. You dare set up to be my father! Thank heaven Ive not a drop of your vile blood in my veins.

TARLETON. (*sitting down again with a shrug*) Well, if you wont be civil, theres no pleasure in talking to you, is there? What do you want? Money?

THE MAN. How dare you insult me?

TARLETON. Well, what d o you want?

THE MAN. Justice.

TARLETON. Youre quite sure thats all?

THE MAN. It's enough for me.

TARLETON. A modest sort of demand, isnt it? Nobody ever had it since the world began, fortunately for themselves; but you must have it, must you? Well, youve come to the wrong shop for it; youll get no justice here: we dont keep it. Human nature is what we stock.

THE MAN. Human nature! Debauchery! gluttony! selfishness! robbery of the poor! Is that what you call human nature?

TARLETON. No: thats what y o u call it. Come, my lad! Whats the matter with you? You dont look starved; and youve a decent suit of clothes.

THE MAN. Forty-two shillings.

TARLETON. They can do you a very decent suit for forty-two shillings. Have you paid for it?

THE MAN. Do you take me for a thief? And do you suppose I can get credit like you?

TARLETON. Then you were able to lay your hand on forty-two shillings. Judging from your conversational style, I should think you must spend at least a shilling a week on romantic literature.

THE MAN. Where would I get a shilling a week to spend on books when I can hardly keep myself decent? I get books at the Free Library.

TARLETON. (*springing to his feet*) What!!!

THE MAN. (*recoiling before his vehemence*) The Free Library. Theres no harm in that.

TARLETON. Ingrate! I supply you with free books; and the use you make of them is to persuade yourself that it's a fine thing to shoot me. (*He throws himself doggedly back into his chair*) I'll never give another penny to a Free Library.

THE MAN. Youll never give another penny to anything. This is the end: for you and me.

TARLETON. Pooh! Come, come, man! talk business. Whats wrong? Are you out of employment?

THE MAN. No. This is my Saturday afternoon. Dont flatter yourself that I'm a loafer or a criminal. I'm a cashier; and I defy you to say that my cash has ever been a farthing wrong. I've a right to call you to account because my hands are clean.

TARLETON. Well, call away. What have I to account for? Had you a hard time with your mother? Why didnt she ask me for money?

THE MAN. She'd have died first. Besides, who wanted your money? Do you suppose we lived in the gutter? My father maynt have been in as large a way as you; but he was better connected; and his shop was as respectable as yours.

TARLETON. I suppose your mother brought him a little capital.

THE MAN. I don't know. Whats that got to do with you?

TARLETON. Well, you say she and I knew one another and parted. She must have had something off me then, you know. One doesnt get out of these things for nothing. Hang it, young man: do you suppose Ive no heart? Of course she had her due; and she found a husband with it, and set him up in business with it, and brought you up respectably; so what the devil have you to complain of?

THE MAN. Are women to be ruined with impunity?

TARLETON. I havnt ruined any woman that I'm aware of. Ive been the making of you and your mother.

THE MAN. Oh, I'm a fool to listen to you and argue with you. I came here to kill you and then kill myself.

TARLETON. Begin with yourself, if you don't mind. Ive a good deal of business to do still before I die. Havnt you?

THE MAN. No. Thats just it: I've no business to do. Do you know what my life is? I spend my days from nine to six—n'ne hours of daylight and fresh air—in a stuffy little den counting another man's money. Ive an intellect: a mind and a brain and a soul; and the use he makes of them is to fix them on his tuppences and his eighteenpences and his two pound seventeen and tenpences and see how much they come to at the end of the day and take care that no one steals them. I enter and enter, and add and add, and take money and give change, and fill cheques and stamp receipts, and not a penny of that money is my own: not one of those transactions has the smallest interest for me or anyone else in the world but him; and even he couldnt stand it if he had to do it all himself. And I'm envied: aye, envied for the variety and liveliness of my job, by the poor devil of a bookkeeper that has to copy all my entries over again. Fifty thousand entries a year that poor wretch makes; and not ten out of the fifty thousand ever has to be referred to again; and when all the figures are counted up and the balance sheet made out, the boss isnt a penny the richer than he'd be if bookkeeping had never been invented. Of all the damnable waste of human life that ever was invented, clerking is the very worst.

TARLETON. Why not join the territorials?

THE MAN. Because the boss wont let me. He hasnt the sense to see that it would pay him to get some cheap soldiering out of me. How can a man tied to a desk from nine to six be anything—be even a man, let alone a soldier? But I'll teach him and you a lesson. Ive had enough of living a dog's life and despising myself for it. Ive had enough of being talked down to by hogs like you, and wearing my life out for a salary that wouldnt keep you in cigars. Youll never believe that a clerk's a man until one of u s makes an example of one of y o u.

TARLETON. Despotism tempered by assassination, eh?

THE MAN. Yes. Thats what they do in Russia. Well, a business office is Russia as far as the clerks are concerned. So dont you take it so coolly. You think I'm not going to do it; but I am.

TARLETON. (*rising and facing him*) Come, now, as man to man! It's not my fault that youre poorer than I am, and it's not your fault that I'm richer than you. And if you could undo all that passed between me and your mother, you wouldn't undo it; and neither would she. But youre sick of your slavery; and you want to be the hero of a romance and to get into the papers. Eh? A son revenges his mother's shame. Villain weltering in his gore. Mother: look down from heaven and receive your unhappy son's last sigh.

THE MAN. Oh, rot! do you think I read novelettes? And do you suppose I believe such superstitions as heaven? I go to church because the boss told me I'd get the sack if I didnt. Free England! Ha! (LINA *appears at the pavilion door, and comes swiftly and noiselessly forward on seeing the man with a pistol in his hand*).

TARLETON. Youre afraid of getting the sack; but youre not afraid to shoot yourself.

THE MAN. Damn you! youre trying to keep me talking until somebody comes. (*He raises the pistol desperately, but not very resolutely*).

LINA. (*at his right elbow*) Somebody h a s come.

THE MAN. (*turning on her*). Stand off. I'll shoot you if you lay a hand on me. I will, by God.

LINA. You cant cover me with that pistol. Try. (*He tries, presenting the pistol at her face. She moves round him in the opposite direction to the hands of a clock with a light dancing step. He finds it impossible to cover her with the pistol: she is always too far to his left.* TARLETON, *behind him, grips his wrist and drags his arm straight up, so that the pistol points to the ceiling. As he tries to turn on his assailant,* LINA *grips his other wrist*) Please stop. I cant bear to twist anyone's wrist; but I must if you dont let the pistol go.

THE MAN. (*letting* TARLETON *take it from him*) All right: I'm done. Couldnt even do that job decently. Thats a clerk all over. Very well: send for your damned police and make an end of it. I'm accustomed to prison from nine to six: I daresay I can stand it from six to nine as well.

TARLETON. Dont swear. Thats a lady. (*He throws the pistol on the writing table*).

THE MAN. (*looking at* LINA *in amazement*) Beaten by a female! It needed only this. (*He collapses in the chair near the worktable, and hides his face. They cannot help pitying him*).

LINA. Old pal: dont call the police. Lend him a bicycle and let him get away.

THE MAN. I cant ride a bicycle. I never could afford one. I'm not even that much good.

TARLETON. If I gave you a hundred pound note now to go and have a good spree with, I wonder would you know how to set about it. Do you ever take a holiday?

THE MAN. Take! I g o t four days last August.

TARLETON. What did you do?

THE MAN. I did a cheap trip to Folkestone. I spent sevenpence on dropping pennies into silly automatic machines and peep-shows of rowdy girls having a jolly time. I spent a penny on the lift and fourpence on refreshments. That cleaned me out. The rest of the time I was so miserable that I was glad to get back to the office. Now you know.

LINA. Come to the gymnasium: I'll teach you how to make a man of yourself. (THE MAN *is about to rise irresolutely, from the mere habit of doing what he is told, when* TARLETON *stops him*).

TARLETON. Young man: dont. Youve tried to shoot me; but I'm not vindictive. I draw the line at putting a man on the rack. If you want every joint in your body stretched until it's an agony to live—until you have an unnatural feeling that all your muscles are singing and laughing with pain—then go to the gymnasium with that lady. But youll be more comfortable in jail.

LINA. (*greatly amused.*) Was that why you went away, old pal? Was that the telegram you said you had forgotten to send? (MRS TARLETON *comes in hastily through the inner door*).

MRS TARLETON. (*on the steps*) Is anything the matter, John? Nurse says she heard you calling me a quarter of an hour ago; and that your voice sounded as if you were ill. (*She comes between* TARLETON *and* THE MAN) Is anything the matter?

TARLETON. This is the son of an old friend of mine. Mr—er—Mr Gunner. (*To the man, who rises awkwardly*) My wife.

MRS TARLETON. Good evening to you.

GUNNER. Er— (*He is too nervous to speak, and makes a shambling bow*).

BENTLEY *looks in at the pavilion door, very peevish, and too preoccupied with his own affairs to pay any attention to those of the company.*

BENTLEY. I say: has anybody seen Hypatia? She promised to come out with me; and I cant find her anywhere. And wheres Joey?

GUNNER. (*suddenly breaking out aggressively, being incapable of any middle way between submissiveness and violence*) *I* can tell you where Hypatia is. I can tell you where Joey is. And I say it's a scandal and an infamy. If people only knew what goes on in this so-called respectable house it would be put a stop to. These are the morals of our pious capitalist class! This is your rotten bourgeoisie! This—

MRS TARLETON. Dont you dare use such language in company. I wont allow it.

TARLETON. All right, Chickabiddy: it's not bad language: it's only Socialism.

MRS TARLETON. Well, I wont have any Socialism in my house.

TARLETON. (*to* GUNNER) You hear what Mrs Tarleton says. Well, in this house everybody does what she says or out they go.

GUNNER. Do you suppose I want to stay? Do you think I would breathe this polluted atmosphere a moment longer than I could help?

BENTLEY. (*running forward between* LINA *and* GUNNER) But what did you mean by what you said about Miss Tarleton and Mr Percival, you beastly rotter, you?

GUNNER. (*to* TARLETON) Oh! is Hypatia your daughter? And Joey is M i s t e r Percival, is he? One of your set, I suppose. One of the smart set! One of the bridge-playing, eighty-horse-power, week-ender set! One of the johnnies I slave for! Well, Joey has more decency than your daughter, anyhow. The women are the worst. I never believed it til I saw it with my own eyes. Well, it won't last for ever. The writing is on the wall. Rome fell. Babylon fell. Hindhead's turn will come.

MRS TARLETON. (*naïvely looking at the wall for the writing*) Whatever are you talking about, young man?

GUNNER. I know what I'm talking about. I went into that Turkish bath a boy: I came out a man.

MRS TARLETON. Good gracious! he's mad. (*To* LINA) Did John make him take a Turkish bath?

LINA. No. He doesnt need Turkish baths: he needs to put on a little flesh. I don't understand what it's all about. I found him trying to shoot Mr Tarleton.

MRS TARLETON. (*with a scream*) Oh! and John encouraging him, I'll be bound! Bunny: you go for the *police.* (*To* GUNNER) I'll teach you to come into my house and shoot my husband.

GUNNER. Teach away. I never asked to be let off. I'm

ashamed to be free instead of taking my part with the rest. Women—beautiful women of noble birth—are going to prison for their opinions. Girl students in Russia go to the gallows; let themselves be cut in pieces with the knout, or driven through the frozen snows of Siberia, sooner than stand looking on tamely at the world being made a hell for the toiling millions. If you were not all skunks and cowards youd be suffering with them instead of battening here on the plunder of the poor.

MRS TARLETON. (*much vexed*) Oh, did you ever hear such silly nonsense? Bunny: go and tell the gardener to send over one of his men to Grayshott for the police.

GUNNER. I'll go with him. I intend to give myself up. I'm going to expose what Ive seen here, no matter what the consequences may be to my miserable self.

TARLETON. Stop. You stay where you are, Ben. Chickabiddy: youve never had the police in. If you had, youd not be in a hurry to have them in again. Now, young man: cut the cackle; and tell us, as short as you can, what did you see?

GUNNER. I cant tell you in the presence of ladies.

MRS TARLETON. Oh, you a r e tiresome. As if it mattered to anyone what you saw. Me! A married woman that might be your mother. (*To* LINA) And I'm sure y o u r e not particular, if youll excuse my saying so.

TARLETON. Out with it. What did you see?

GUNNER. I saw your daughter with my own eyes—oh well, never mind what I saw.

BENTLEY. (*almost crying with anxiety*) You beastly rotter. I'll get Joey to give you such a hiding—

TARLETON. You cant leave it at that, you know. What did you see my daughter doing?

GUNNER. After all, why shouldnt she do it? The Russian students do it. Women should be as free as men. I'm a fool. I'm so full of your bourgeois morality that I let myself be shocked by the application of my own revolutionary principles. If she likes the man why shouldnt she tell him so?

MRS TARLETON. I do wonder at you, John, letting him talk like this before everybody. (*Turning rather tartly to* LINA) Would you mind going away to the drawing room just for a few minutes, Miss Chipenoska. This is a private family matter, if you dont mind.

LINA. I should have gone before, Mrs Tarleton, if there had been anyone to protect Mr Tarleton and the young gentleman. (*She goes out through the inner door*).

GUNNER. There you are! It's all of a piece here. The men effeminate, the women unsexed—

TARLETON. Dont begin again, old chap. Keep it for Trafalgar Square.

HYPATIA'S VOICE OUTSIDE. No, no. (*She breaks off in a stifled half laugh, half scream, and is seen darting across the garden with* PERCIVAL *in hot pursuit. Immediately afterwards she appears again, and runs into the pavilion. Finding it full of people, including a stranger, she stops; but* PERCIVAL, *flushed and reckless, rushes in and seizes her before he, too, realizes that they are not alone. He releases her in confusion. Dead silence. They are all afraid to look at one another except* MRS TARLETON, *who stares sternly at* HYPATIA. HYPATIA *is the first to recover her presence of mind*) Excuse me rushing in like this. Mr Percival has been chasing me down the hill.

GUNNER. Who chased him up it? Dont be ashamed. Be fearless. Be truthful.

TARLETON. Gunner: will you go to Paris for a fortnight? I'll pay your expenses.

HYPATIA. What do you mean?

GUNNER. There was a silent witness in the Turkish bath.

TARLETON. I found him hiding there. Whatever went on here, he saw and heard. Thats what he means.

PERCIVAL. (*sternly approaching* GUNNER, *and speaking with deep but contained indignation*) Am I to understand you as daring to put forward the monstrous and blackguardly lie that this lady behaved improperly in my presence?

GUNNER. (*turning white*) You know what I saw and heard.

HYPATIA, *with a gleam of triumph in her eyes, slips noiselessly into the swing chair, and watches* PERCIVAL *and* GUNNER, *swinging slightly, but otherwise motionless.*

PERCIVAL. I hope it is not necessary for me to assure you all that there is not one word of truth—not one grain of substance—in this rascally calumny, which no man with a spark of decent feeling would have uttered even if he had been ignorant enough to believe it. Miss Tarleton's conduct, since I have had the honor of knowing her, has been, I need hardly say, in every respect beyond reproach. (*To* GUNNER) As for you, sir, youll have the goodness to come out with me immediately. I have some business with you which cant be settled in Mrs Tarleton's presence or in her house.

GUNNER. (*painfully frightened*) Why should I go out with you?

PERCIVAL. Because I intend that you shall.

GUNNER. I wont be bullied by you. (PERCIVAL *makes a threatening step towards him*) Police! (*He tries to bolt; but* PERCIVAL *seizes him*) Leave me go, will you? What right have you to lay hands on me?

TARLETON. Let him run for it, Mr Percival. He's very poor company. We shall be well rid of him. Let him go.

PERCIVAL. Not until he has taken back and made the fullest apology for the abominable lie he has told. He shall do that, or he shall defend himself as best he can against the most thorough thrashing I'm capable of giving him. (*Releasing* GUNNER, *but facing him ominously*) Take your choice. Which is it to be?

GUNNER. Give me a fair chance. Go and stick at a desk from nine to six for a month, and let me have your grub and your sport and your lessons in boxing, and I'll fight you fast enough. You know I'm no good or you darent bully me like this.

PERCIVAL. You should have thought of that before you attacked a lady with a dastardly slander. I'm waiting for your decision. I'm rather in a hurry, please.

GUNNER. I never said anything against the lady.

MRS TARLETON. ⎫ Oh, listen to that!
BENTLEY.   ⎪ What a liar!
HYPATIA.   ⎬ Oh!
TARLETON.   ⎭ Oh, come!

PERCIVAL. We'll have it in writing, if you dont mind. (*Pointing to the writing table*) Sit down; and take that pen in your hand. (GUNNER *looks irresolutely a little way round; then obeys*) Now write. "I," whatever your name is—

GUNNER. (*after a vain attempt*) I cant. My hand's shaking too much. You see it's no use. I'm doing my best. I cant.

PERCIVAL. Mr Summerhays will write it: you can sign it.

BENTLEY. (*insolently to* GUNNER) Get up. (GUNNER *obeys; and* BENTLEY, *shouldering him aside towards* PERCIVAL, *takes his place and prepares to write*).

PERCIVAL. Whats your name?

GUNNER. John Brown.

TARLETON. Oh come! Couldnt you make it Horace Smith? or Algernon Robinson?

GUNNER. (*agitatedly*). But my name i s John Brown. There a r e really John Browns. How can I help it if my name's a common one?

BENTLEY. Shew us a letter addressed to you.

GUNNER. How can I! I never get any letters: I'm only a clerk. I can shew you J. B. on my handkerchief. (*He takes out a not very clean one*).

BENTLEY. (*with disgust*). Oh, put it up again. Let it go at John Brown.

PERCIVAL. Where do you live?

GUNNER. 4 Chesterfield Parade, Kentish Town, N.W.

PERCIVAL. (*dictating*) I, John Brown, of 4 Chesterfield Parade, Kentish Town, do hereby voluntarily con-

fess that on the 31st May 1909 I— (*To* TARLETON)
What did he do exactly?

TARLETON. (*dictating*) —I trespassed on the land of
John Tarleton at Hindhead, and effected an unlawful
entry into his house, where I secreted myself in a portable Turkish bath—

BENTLEY. Go slow, old man. Just a moment. "Turkish
bath"—yes?

TARLETON. (*continuing*). —with a pistol, with which
I threatened to take the life of the said John Tarleton—

MRS TARLETON. Oh, John! You might have been killed.

TARLETON. —and was prevented from doing so only
by the timely arrival of the celebrated Miss Lina
Szczepanowska.

MRS TARLETON. Is she celebrated? (*Apologetically*)
I never dreamt—

BENTLEY. Look here: I'm awfully sorry; but I cant
spell Szczepanowska.

PERCIVAL. I think it's S, z, c, z—Better say the Polish
lady.

BENTLEY. (*writing*) "the Polish lady"?

TARLETON. (*to* PERCIVAL) Now it's your turn.

PERCIVAL. (*dictating*) I further confess that I was
guilty of uttering an abominable calumny concerning
Miss Hypatia Tarleton, for which there was not a shred
of foundation.

Impressive silence whilst BENTLEY *writes.*

BENTLEY. "foundation"?

PERCIVAL. I apologize most humbly to the lady and
her family for my conduct— (*He waits for* BENTLEY *to
write*).

BENTLEY. "conduct"?

PERCIVAL. —and I promise Mr Tarleton not to repeat
it, and to amend my life—

BENTLEY. "amend my life"?

PERCIVAL. —and to do what in me lies to prove worthy
of his kindness in giving me another chance—

BENTLEY. "another chance"?

PERCIVAL. —and refraining from delivering me up to the punishment I so richly deserve.

BENTLEY. "richly deserve."

PERCIVAL. (*to* HYPATIA) Does that satisfy you, Miss Tarleton?

HYPATIA. Yes: that will teach him to tell lies next time.

BENTLEY. (*rising to make place for* GUNNER *and handing him the pen*) You mean it will teach him to tell the truth next time.

TARLETON. Ahem! Do you, Patsy?

PERCIVAL. Be good enough to sign. (GUNNER *sits down helplessly and dips the pen in the ink*) I hope what you are signing is no mere form of words to you, and that you not only say you are sorry, but that you a r e sorry. (LORD SUMMERHAYS *and* JOHNNY *come in through the pavilion door*).

MRS TARLETON. Stop. Mr Percival: I think, on Hypatia's account, Lord Summerhays ought to be told about this.

LORD SUMMERHAYS, *wondering what the matter is, comes forward between* PERCIVAL *and* BENTLEY. JOHNNY *stops beside* HYPATIA.

PERCIVAL. Certainly.

TARLETON. (*uneasily*) Take my advice and cut it short. Get rid of him.

MRS TARLETON. Hypatia ought to have her character cleared.

TARLETON. You let well enough alone, Chickabiddy. Most of our characters will bear a little careful dusting; but they wont bear scouring. Patsy is jolly well out of it. What does it matter, anyhow?

PERCIVAL. Mr Tarleton: we have already said either too much or not enough. Lord Summerhays: will you be kind enough to witness the declaration this man has just signed?

GUNNER. I havnt yet. Am I to sign now?

PERCIVAL. Of course. (GUNNER, *who is now incapable of doing anything on his own initiative, signs*) Now stand

up and read your declaration to this gentleman. (GUN-
NER *makes a vague movement and looks stupidly round.*
PERCIVAL *adds peremptorily*) Now, please.

GUNNER. (*rising apprehensively and reading without
punctuation in a hardly audible voice, like a very sick
man*) I John Brown of 4 Chesterfield Parade Kentish
Town do hereby voluntarily confess that on the 31st
May 1909 I trespassed on the land of John Tarleton
at Hindhead and effected an unlawful entry into his
house where I secreted myself in a portable Turkish
bath with a pistol with which I threatened to take the
life of the said John Tarleton and was prevented from
doing so only by the timely arrival of the Polish lady I
further confess that I was guilty of uttering an abominable calumny concerning Miss Hypatia Tarleton for which
there was not a shred of foundation I apologize most
humbly to the lady and her family for my conduct and
I promise Mr Tarleton not to repeat it and to amend my
life and to do what in me lies to prove worthy of his
kindness in giving me another chance and refraining
from delivering me up to the punishment I so richly
deserve.

A short and painful silence follows. Then PERCIVAL
speaks.

PERCIVAL. Do you consider that sufficient, Lord Summerhays?

LORD SUMMERHAYS. Oh quite, quite.

PERCIVAL. (*to* HYPATIA) Lord Summerhays would
probably like to hear you say that you are satisfied,
Miss Tarleton.

HYPATIA. (*coming out of the swing, and advancing
between* PERCIVAL *and* LORD SUMMERHAYS) I must say
that you have behaved like a perfect gentleman, Mr
Percival.

PERCIVAL. (*first bowing to* HYPATIA, *and then turning
with cold contempt to* GUNNER, *who is standing helpless*) We need not trouble you any further. (GUNNER
turns vaguely towards the pavilion).

JOHNNY. (*with less refined offensiveness, pointing to*

the pavilion) Thats your way. The gardener will shew you the shortest way into the road. Go the shortest way.

GUNNER. (*oppressed and disconcerted, hardly knows how to get out of the room*) Yes, sir. I— (*He turns again, appealing to* TARLETON.) Maynt I have my mother's photographs back again? (MRS TARLETON *pricks up her ears*).

TARLETON. Eh? What? Oh, the photographs! Yes, yes, yes: take them. (GUNNER *takes them from the table, and is creeping away, when* MRS TARLETON *puts out her hand and stops him*).

MRS TARLETON. Whats this, John? What were you doing with his mother's photographs?

TARLETON. Nothing, nothing. Never mind, Chickabiddy: it's all right.

MRS TARLETON. (*snatching the photographs from* GUNNER'S *irresolute fingers, and recognizing them at a glance*) Lucy Titmus! Oh John, John!

TARLETON. (*grimly, to* GUNNER) Young man: youre a fool; but youve just put the lid on this job in a masterly manner. I knew you would. I told you all to let well alone. You wouldnt; and now you must take the consequences—or rather *I* must take them.

MRS TARLETON. (*maternally*) Are you Lucy's son?

GUNNER. Yes!

MRS TARLETON. And why didnt you come to me? I didnt turn my back on your mother when she came to me in her trouble. Didnt you know that?

GUNNER. No. She never talked to me about anything.

TARLETON. How could she talk to her own son? Shy, Summerhays, shy. Parent and child. Shy. (*He sits down at the end of the writing table nearest the sideboard like a man resigned to anything that fate may have in store for him*).

MRS TARLETON. Then how did you find out?

GUNNER. From her papers after she died.

MRS TARLETON. (*shocked*) Is Lucy dead? And I never knew! (*With an effusion of tenderness*) And you

here being treated like that, poor orphan, with nobody
to take your part! Tear up that foolish paper, child; and
sit down and make friends with me.

JOHNNY.   Hallo, mother: this is all very well, you
            know—

PERCIVAL.   But may I point out, Mrs Tarleton,
            that—

BENTLEY.   Do you mean that after what he said
            of—

HYPATIA.   Oh, look here, mamma: this is really—

MRS TARLETON. Will you please speak one at a time?
Silence.

PERCIVAL. (*in a very gentlemanly manner*) Will you
allow me to remind you, Mrs Tarleton, that this man
has uttered a most serious and disgraceful falsehood
concerning Miss Tarleton and myself?

MRS TARLETON. I dont believe a word of it. If the
poor lad was there in the Turkish bath, who has a better
right to say what was going on here than he has? You
ought to be ashamed of yourself, Patsy: and so ought
you too, Mr Percival, for encouraging her. (HYPATIA
retreats to the pavilion, and exchanges grimaces with
JOHNNY, *shamelessly enjoying* PERCIVAL'S *sudden reverse. They know their mother*).

PERCIVAL. (*gasping*) Mrs Tarleton: I give you my
word of honor—

MRS TARLETON. Oh, go along with you and your word
of honor. Do you think I'm a fool? I wonder you can look
the lad in the face after bullying him and making him
sign those wicked lies; and all the time you carrying on
with my daughter before youd been half an hour in my
house. Fie, for shame!

PERCIVAL. Lord Summerhays: I appeal to you. Have
I done the correct thing or not?

LORD SUMMERHAYS. Youve done your best, Mr
Percival. But the correct thing depends for its success
on everybody playing the game very strictly. As a single-
handed game, it's impossible.

BENTLEY. (*suddenly breaking out lamentably*) Joey: have you taken Hypatia away from me?

LORD SUMMERHAYS. (*severely*) Bentley! Bentley! Control yourself, sir.

TARLETON. Come, Mr Percival! the shutters are up on the gentlemanly business. Try the truth.

PERCIVAL. I am in a wretched position. If I tell the truth nobody will believe me.

TARLETON. Oh yes they will. The truth makes everybody believe it.

PERCIVAL. It also makes everybody pretend not to believe it. Mrs Tarleton: youre not playing the game.

MRS TARLETON. I dont think youve behaved at all nicely, Mr Percival.

BENTLEY. I wouldnt have played you such a dirty trick, Joey. (*Struggling with a sob*) You beast.

LORD SUMMERHAYS. Bentley: you m u s t control yourself. Let me say at the same time, Mr Percival, that my son seems to have been mistaken in regarding you either as his friend or as a gentleman.

PERCIVAL. Miss Tarleton: I'm suffering this for your sake. I ask you just to say that I am not to blame. Just that and nothing more.

HYPATIA. (*gloating mischievously over his distress*) You chased me through the heather and kissed me. You shouldnt have done that if you were not in earnest.

PERCIVAL. Oh, this is really the limit. (*Turning desperately to* GUNNER) Sir: I appeal to y o u. As a gentleman! as a man of honor! as a man bound to stand by another man! You were in that Turkish bath. You saw how it began. Could any man have behaved more correctly than I did? Is there a shadow of foundation for the accusations brought against me?

GUNNER. (*sorely perplexed*) Well, what do you want me to say?

JOHNNY. He has said what he had to say already, hasnt he? Read that paper.

GUNNER. When I tell the truth, you make me go back

on it. And now you want me to go back on myself! What is a man to do?

PERCIVAL. (*patiently*) Please try to get your mind clear, Mr Brown. I pointed out to you that you could not, as a gentleman, disparage a lady's character. You agree with me, I hope.

GUNNER. Yes: that sounds all right.

PERCIVAL. But youre also bound to tell the truth. Surely youll not deny that.

GUNNER. Who's denying it? I say nothing against it.

PERCIVAL. Of course not. Well, I ask you to tell the truth simply and unaffectedly. Did you witness any improper conduct on my part when you were in the bath?

GUNNER. No, sir.

JOHNNY.   ⎞ Then what do you mean by saying that—
HYPATIA.   ⎬ Do you mean to say that I—
BENTLEY.   ⎠ Oh, you a r e a rotter. Youre afraid—

TARLETON. (*rising*) Stop. (*Silence*) Leave it at that. Enough said. You keep quiet, Johnny. Mr Percival: youre whitewashed. So are you, Patsy. Honors are easy. Lets drop the subject. The next thing to do is to open a subscription to start this young man on a ranch in some far country thats accustomed to be in a disturbed state. He—

MRS TARLETON. Now stop joking the poor lad, John: I wont have it. He's been worried to death between you all. (*To* GUNNER) Have you had your tea?

GUNNER. Tea? No: it's too early. I'm all right; only I had no dinner: I didn't think I'd want it. I didn't think I'd be alive.

MRS TARLETON. Oh, what a thing to say! You mustnt talk like that.

JOHNNY. He's out of his mind. He thinks it's past dinner-time.

MRS TARLETON. Oh, youve no sense, Johnny. He calls his lunch his dinner, and has his tea at half-past six. Havnt you, dear?

GUNNER. (*timidly*) Hasnt everybody?

JOHNNY. (*laughing*) Well, by George, thats not bad.

MRS TARLETON. Now dont be rude, Johnny: you know I dont like it. (*To* GUNNER) A cup of tea will pick you up.

GUNNER. I'd rather not. I'm all right.

TARLETON. (*going to the sideboard*) Here! try a mouthful of sloe gin.

GUNNER. No, thanks, I'm a teetotaler. I cant touch alcohol in any form.

TARLETON. Nonsense! This isnt alcohol. Sloe gin. Vegetarian, you know.

GUNNER. (*hesitating*) Is it a fruit beverage?

TARLETON. Of course it is. Fruit beverage. Here you are. (*He gives him a glass of sloe gin*).

GUNNER. (*going to the sideboard*) Thanks. (*He begins to drink it confidently; but the first mouthful startles and almost chokes him*) It's rather hot.

TARLETON. Do you good. Dont be afraid of it.

MRS TARLETON. (*going to him*) Sip it, dear. Dont be in a hurry.

GUNNER *sips slowly, each sip making his eyes water.*

JOHNNY. (*coming forward into the place left vacant by* GUNNER'S *visit to the sideboard*) Well, now that the gentleman has been attended to, I should like to know where we are. It may be a vulgar business habit; but I confess I like to know where I am.

TARLETON. I dont. Wherever you are, youre there anyhow. I tell you again, leave it at that.

BENTLEY. I want to know too. Hypatia's engaged to me.

HYPATIA. Bentley: if you insult me again: if you say another word, I'll leave the house and not enter it until you leave it.

JOHNNY. Put that in your pipe and smoke it, my boy.

BENTLEY. (*inarticulate with fury and suppressed tears*) Oh! Beasts! Brutes!

MRS TARLETON. Now dont hurt his feelings, poor little lamb!

LORD SUMMERHAYS. (*very sternly*) Bentley: you are not behaving well. You had better leave us until you have recovered yourself.

BENTLEY *goes out in disgrace, but gets no further than half-way to the pavilion door, when, with a wild sob, he throws himself on the floor and begins to yell.*

MRS TARLETON.	(*running to him*) Oh, poor child, poor child! Dont cry, duckie: he didnt mean it: dont cry.
LORD SUMMER-HAYS.	Stop that infernal noise, sir: do you hear? Stop it instantly.
JOHNNY.	Thats the game he tried on me. There you are! Now, mother! Now, Patsy! You see for yourselves.
HYPATIA.	(*covering her ears*) Oh you little wretch! Stop him, Mr Percival. Kick him.
TARLETON.	Steady on, steady on. Easy, Bunny, easy.

LINA. (*appearing at the door*) Leave him to me, Mrs Tarleton. (*Clear and uthoritative*) Stand clear, please.

She quickly lifts the upper half of BENTLEY *from the ground; dives under him; rises with his body hanging across her shoulders; and runs out with him.*

BENTLEY. (*in scared, sobered, humble tones as he is borne off*) What are you doing? Let me down. Please, Miss Szczepanowska—* (They pass out of hearing*).

An awestruck silence falls on the company as they speculate on BENTLEY'S *fate.*

JOHNNY. I wonder what she's going to do with him.

HYPATIA. Spank him, I hope. Spank him hard.

LORD SUMMERHAYS. I hope so. I hope so. Tarleton: I'm beyond measure humiliated and annoyed by my son's behavior in your house. I had better take him home.

TARLETON. Not at all: not at all. Now, Chickabiddy:

as Miss Lina has taken away Ben, suppose you take away Mr Brown for a while.

GUNNER. (*with unexpected aggressiveness*) My name isnt Brown. (*They stare at him: he meets their stare defiantly, pugnacious with sloe gin; drains the last drop from his glass; throws it on the sideboard; and advances to the writing table*) My name's Baker: Julius Baker. M i s t e r Baker. If any man doubts it, I'm ready for him.

MRS TARLETON. John: you shouldnt have given him that sloe gin. It's gone to his head.

GUNNER. Dont you think it. Fruit beverages dont go to the head; and what matter if they did? I say nothing to you, maam: I regard you with respect and affection. (*Lachrymosely*) You were very good to my mother: my poor mother! (*Relapsing into his daring mood*) But I say my name's Baker; and I'm not to be treated as a child or made a slave of by any man. Baker is my name. Did you think I was going to give you my real name? Not likely! Not me!

TARLETON. So you thought of John Brown. That w a s clever of you.

GUNNER. Clever! Yes: we're not all such fools as you think: we clerks. It was the bookkeeper put me up to that. It's the only name that nobody gives as a false name, he said. Clever, eh? I should think so.

MRS TARLETON. Come now, Julius—

GUNNER. (*reassuring her gravely*) Dont you be alarmed, maam. I know what is due to you as a lady and to myself as a gentleman. I regard you with respect and affection. If you had been my mother, as you ought to have been, I should have had more chance. But you shall have no cause to be ashamed of me. The strength of a chain is no greater than its weakest link; but the greatness of a poet is the greatness of his greatest moment. Shakespear used to get drunk. Frederick the Great ran away from a battle. But it was what they could rise to, not what they could sink to, that made them great. They werent good always; but they were good on their day. Well, on my day—on my day, mind you—I'm good for something too. I know that Ive made a silly exhibition of myself here. I know I didn't rise to the occasion. I know that if youd been my mother, youd have been ashamed of me. I lost my presence of mind: I was a contemptible coward. But (*Slapping himself on the chest*) I'm not the man I was then. This is my day. Ive seen the tenth possessor of a foolish face carried out kicking and screaming by a woman. (*To* PERCIVAL) Y o u crowed pretty big over me. You hypnotized me. But when you were put through the fire yourself, you were found wanting. I tell you straight I dont give a damn for you.

MRS TARLETON. No: thats naughty. You shouldnt say that before me.

GUNNER. I would cut my tongue out sooner than say anything vulgar in your presence; for I regard you with respect and affection. I was not swearing. I was affirming my manhood.

MRS TARLETON. What an idea! What puts all these things into your head?

GUNNER. Oh, dont think, because I'm only a clerk, that I'm not one of the intellectuals. I'm a reading man, a thinking man. I read in a book—a high class six shilling book—this precept: Affirm your manhood. It appealed to me. Ive always remembered it. I believe in it. I feel I must do it to recover your respect after my cowardly behavior. Therefore I affirm it in your presence. I tell that man who insulted me that I dont give a damn for him. And neither I do.

TARLETON. I say, Summerhays: did you have chaps of this sort in Jinghiskahn?

LORD SUMMERHAYS. Oh yes: they exist everywhere: they are a most serious modern problem.

GUNNER. Yes. Youre right. (*Conceitedly*) I'm a problem. And I tell you that when we clerks realize that we're problems! well, look out: thats all.

LORD SUMMERHAYS. (*suavely, to* GUNNER) You read a great deal, you say?

GUNNER. Ive read more than any man in this room, if the truth were known, I expect. Thats whats going to smash up your Capitalism. The problems are beginning to read. Ha! We're free to do that here in England. What would you do with me in Jinghiskahn if you had me there?

LORD SUMMERHAYS. Well, since you ask me so directly, I'll tell you. I should take advantage of the fact that you have neither sense enough nor strength enough to know how to behave yourself in a difficulty of any sort. I should warn an intelligent and ambitious policeman that you are a troublesome person. The intelligent and ambitious policeman would take an early opportunity of upsetting your temper by ordering you to move on, and treading on your heels until you were provoked into obstructing an officer in the discharge of his duty. Any trifle of that sort would be sufficient to make a man like you lose your self-possession and put yourself in the wrong. You would then be charged and imprisoned until things quieted down.

GUNNER. And you call that justice!

LORD SUMMERHAYS. No. Justice was not my business. I had to govern a province; and I took the necessary steps to maintain order in it. Men are not governed by justice, but by law or persuasion. When they refuse to be governed by law or persuasion, they have to be governed by force or fraud, or both. I used both when law and persuasion failed me. Every ruler of men since the world began has done so, even when he has hated both fraud and force as heartily as I do. It is as well that you should know this, my young friend; so that you may recognize in time that anarchism is a game at which the police can beat you. What have you to say to that?

GUNNER. What have I to say to it! Well, I call it scandalous: thats what I have to say to it.

LORD SUMMERHAYS. Precisely: thats all anybody has

to say to it, except the British public, which pretends not to believe it. And now let me ask you a sympathetic personal question. Havnt you a headache?

GUNNER. Well, since you ask me, I have. Ive overexcited myself.

MRS TARLETON. Poor lad! No wonder, after all youve gone through! You want to eat a little and to lie down. You come with me. I want you to tell me about your poor dear mother and about yourself. Come along with me. (*She leads the way to the inner door*).

GUNNER. (*following her obediently*) Thank you kindly, madam. (*She goes out. Before passing out after her, he partly closes the door and lingers for a moment to whisper*) Mind: I'm not kuckling down to any man here. I knuckle down to Mrs Tarleton because she's a woman in a thousand. I affirm my manhood all the same. Understand: I dont give a damn for the lot of you. (*He hurries out, rather afraid of the consequences of this defiance, which has provoked* JOHNNY *to an impatient movement towards him*).

HYPATIA. Thank goodness he's gone! Oh, w h a t a bore! WHAT a bore!!! Talk! talk! talk!

TARLETON. Patsy: it's no good. We're going to talk. And we're going to talk about you.

JOHNNY. It's no use shirking it, Pat. We'd better know where we are.

LORD SUMMERHAYS. Come, Miss Tarleton. Wont you sit down? I'm very tired of standing. (HYPATIA *comes from the pavilion and takes a chair at the worktable.* LORD SUMMERHAYS *takes the opposite chair, on her right.* PERCIVAL *takes the chair* JOHNNY *placed for* LINA *on her arrival.* TARLETON *sits down at the end of the writing table.* JOHNNY *remains standing.* LORD SUMMERHAYS *continues, with a sigh of relief at being seated*) We shall now get the change of subject we are all pining for.

JOHNNY. (*puzzled*) Whats that?

LORD SUMMERHAYS. The great question. The question

that men and women will spend hours over without complaining. The question that occupies all the novel readers and all the playgoers. The question they never get tired of.

JOHNNY. But what question?

LORD SUMMERHAYS. The question which particular young man some young woman will mate with.

PERCIVAL. As if it mattered!

HYPATIA. (*sharply*) Whats that you said?

PERCIVAL. I said: As if it mattered.

HYPATIA. I call that ungentlemanly.

PERCIVAL. Do you care about that? you who are so mangificently unladylike!

JOHNNY. Look here, Mr Percival: youre not supposed to insult my sister.

HYPATIA. Oh, shut up, Johnny. I can take care of myself. Dont you interfere.

JOHNNY. Oh, very well, If you choose to give yourself away like that—to allow a man to call you unladylike and then to b e unladylike, Ive nothing more to say.

HYPATIA. I think Mr Percival is most ungentlemanly; but I wont be protected. I'll not have my affairs interfered with by men on pretence of protecting me. I'm not your baby. If I interfered between you and a woman, you would soon tell me to mind my own business.

TARLETON. Children: dont squabble. Read Dr Watts. Behave yourselves.

JOHNNY. Ive nothing more to say; and as I dont seem to be wanted here, I shall take myself off. (*He goes out with affected calm through the pavilion*).

TARLETON. Summerhays: a family is an awful thing, an impossible thing. Cat and dog. Patsy: I'm ashamed of you.

HYPATIA. I'll make it up with Johnny afterwards; but I really cant have him here sticking his clumsy hoof into my affairs.

LORD SUMMERHAYS. The question is, Mr Percival, are you really a gentleman, or are you not?

PERCIVAL. Was Napoleon really a gentleman or was he not? He made the lady get out of the way of the porter and said, "Respect the burden, madam." That was behaving like a very fine gentleman; but he kicked Volney for saying that what France wanted was the Bourbons back again. That was behaving rather like a navvy. Now I, like Napoleon, am not all one piece. On occasion, as you have all seen, I can behave like a gentleman. On occasion, I can behave with a brutal simplicity which Miss Tarleton herself could hardly surpass.

TARLETON. Gentleman or no gentleman, Patsy: what are your intentions?

HYPATIA. My intentions! Surely it's the gentleman who should be asked his intentions.

TARLETON. Come now, Patsy! none of that nonsense. Has Mr Percival said anything to you that I ought to know or that Bentley ought to know? Have you said anything to Mr Percival?

HYPATIA. Mr Percival chased me through the heather and kissed me.

LORD SUMMERHAYS. As a gentleman, Mr Percival, what do you say to that?

PERCIVAL. As a gentleman, I do not kiss and tell. As a mere man: a mere cad, if you like, I say that I did so at Miss Tarleton's own suggestion.

HYPATIA. Beast!

PERCIVAL. I dont deny that I enjoyed it. But I did not initiate it. And I began by running away.

TARLETON. So Patsy can run faster than you, can she?

PERCIVAL. Yes, when she is in pursuit of me. She runs faster and faster. I run slower and slower. And these woods of yours are full of magic. There was a confounded fern owl. Did you ever hear the churr of a fern owl? Did you ever hear it create a sudden silence by ceasing? Did you ever hear it call its mate by striking its wings together twice and whistling that single note that no nightingale can imitate? That is what happened in the woods when I was running away. So I turned; and the pursuer became the pursued.

HYPATIA. I had to fight like a wild cat.

LORD SUMMERHAYS. Please dont tell us this. It's not fit for old people to hear.

TARLETON. Come: how did it end?

HYPATIA. It's not ended yet.

TARLETON. How is it going to end?

HYPATIA. Ask h i m?

TARLETON. How is it going to end, Mr Percival?

PERCIVAL. I cant afford to marry, Mr Tarleton. Ive only a thousand a year until my father dies. Two people cant possibly live on that.

TARLETON. Oh, cant they? When *I* married, I should have been jolly glad to have felt sure of the quarter of it.

PERCIVAL. No doubt; but I am not a cheap person, Mr Tarleton. I was brought up in a household which cost at least seven or eight times that; and I am in constant money difficulties because I simply dont know how to live on the thousand a year scale. As to ask a woman to share my degrading poverty, it's out of the question. Besides, I'm rather young to marry. I'm only 28.

HYPATIA. Papa: buy the brute for me.

LORD SUMMERHAYS. (*shrinking*) My dear Miss Tarleton: dont be so naughty. I know how delightful it is to shock an old man; but there is a point at which it becomes barbarous. Dont. Please dont.

HYPATIA. Shall I tell papa about y o u?

LORD SUMMERHAYS. Tarleton: I had better tell you that I once asked your daughter to become my widow.

TARLETON. (*to* HYPATIA) Why didn't you accept him, you young idiot?

LORD SUMMERHAYS. I was too old.

TARLETON. All this has been going on under my nose, I suppose. You run after young men; and old men run after you. And I'm the last person in the world to hear of it.

HYPATIA. How could I tell you?

Lord Summerhays. Parents and children, Tarleton.

Tarleton. Oh, the gulf that lies between them! the impassable, eternal gulf! And so I'm to buy the brute for you, eh?

Hypatia. If you please, papa.

Tarleton. Whats the price, Mr Percival?

Percival. We might do with another fifteen hundred if my father would contribute. But I should like more.

Tarleton. It's purely a question of money with you, is it?

Percival. (*after a moment's consideration*) Pratically yes: it turns on that.

Tarleton. I thought you might have some sort of preference for Patsy, you know.

Percival. Well, but does that matter, do you think? Patsy fascinates me, no doubt. I apparently fascinate Patsy. But, believe me, all that is not worth considering. One of my three fathers (the priest) has married hundreds of couples: couples selected by one another, couples selected by the parents, couples forced to marry one another by circumstances of one kind or another; and he assures me that if marriages were made by putting all the men's names into one sack and the women's names into another, and having them taken out by a blindfolded child like lottery numbers, there would be just as high a percentage of happy marriages as we have here in England. He said Cupid was nothing but the blindfolded child: pretty idea that, I think! I shall have as good a chance with Patsy as with anyone else. Mind: I'm not bigoted about it. I'm not a doctrinaire: not the slave of a theory. You and Lord Summerhays are experienced married men. If you can tell me of any trustworthy method of selecting a wife, I shall be happy to make use of it. I await your suggestions. (*He looks with polite attention to* Lord Summerhays, *who, having nothing to say, avoids his eye. He looks to* Tarleton, *who purses his lips glumly and rattles his money in his pockets without a word*) Apparently neither of you has anything to suggest. Then Patsy will do as well as another, provided the money is forthcoming.

HYPATIA. Oh, you beauty! You beauty!

TARLETON. When I married Patsy's mother, I was in love with her.

PERCIVAL. For the first time?

TARLETON. Yes: for the first time.

PERCIVAL. For the last time?

LORD SUMMERHAYS. (*revolted*) Sir: you are in the presence of his daughter.

HYPATIA. Oh, dont mind me. I dont care. I'm accustomed to papa's adventures.

TARLETON. (*blushing painfully*) Patsy, my child: that was not—not delicate.

HYPATIA. Well, papa, youve never shewn any delicacy in talking to me about my conduct; and I really dont see why I shouldnt talk to you about yours. It's such nonsense! Do you think young people dont know?

LORD SUMMERHAYS. I'm sure they dont feel. Tarleton: this is too horrible, too brutal. If neither of these young people have any—any—any—

PERCIVAL. Shall we say paternal sentimentality? I'm extremely sorry to shock you; but you must remember that Ive been educated to discuss human affairs with three fathers simultaneously. I'm an adult person. Patsy is an adult person. You do not inspire me with veneration. Apparently you do not inspire Patsy with veneration. That may surprise you. It may pain you. I'm sorry. It cant be helped. What about the money?

TARLETON. You dont inspire me with generosity, young man.

HYPATIA. (*laughing with genuine amusement*) He had you there, Joey.

TARLETON. I havent been a bad father to you, Patsy.

HYPATIA. I dont say you have, dear. If only I could persuade you Ive grown up, we should get along perfectly.

TARLETON. Do you remember Bill Burt?

HYPATIA. Why?

TARLETON. (*to the others*) Bill Burt was a laborer here. I was going to sack him for kicking his father. He said his father had kicked him until he was big enough to kick back. Patsy begged him off. I asked that man what it felt like the first time he kicked his father, and found that it was just like kicking any other man. He laughed and said that it was the old man that knew what it felt like. Think of that, Summerhays! think of that!

HYPATIA. I havnt kicked you, papa.

TARLETON. Youve kicked me harder than Bill Burt ever kicked.

LORD SUMMERHAYS. It's no use, Tarleton. Spare yourself. Do you seriously expect these young people, at their age, to sympathize with what this gentleman calls your paternal sentimentality?

TARLETON. (*wistfully*) Is it nothing to you but paternal sentimentality, Patsy?

HYPATIA. Well, I greatly prefer your superabundant vitality, papa.

TARLETON. (*violently*) Hold your tongue, you young devil. The young are all alike: hard, coarse, shallow, cruel, selfish, dirty-minded. You can clear out of my house as soon as you can coax him to take you; and the sooner the better. (*To* PERCIVAL) I think you said your price was fifteen hundred a year. Take it. And I wish you joy of your bargain.

PERCIVAL. If you wish to know who I am—

TARLETON. I dont care a tinker's curse who you are or what you are. Youre willing to take that girl off my hands for fifteen hundred a year: thats all that concerns me. Tell h e r who you are if you like: it's her affair, not mine.

HYPATIA. Dont answer him, Joey: it wont last. Lord Summerhays, I'm sorry about Bentley; but Joey's the only man for me.

LORD SUMMERHAYS. It may—

HYPATIA. Please dont say it may break your poor boy's heart. It's much more likely to break yours.

LORD SUMMERHAYS. Oh!

TARLETON. (*springing to his feet*) Leave the room. Do you hear: leave the room.

PERCIVAL. Arnt we getting a little cross? Dont be angry, Mr Tarleton. Read Marcus Aurelius.

TARLETON. Dont you dare make fun of me. Take your aeroplane out of my vinery and yourself out of my house.

PERCIVAL. (*rising, to* HYPATIA) I'm afraid I shall have to dine at the Beacon, Patsy.

HYPATIA. (*rising*) Do. I dine with you.

TARLETON. Did you hear me tell you to leave the room?

HYPATIA. I did. (*To* PERCIVAL) You see what living with one's parents means, Joey. It means living in a house where you can be ordered to leave the room. Ive got to obey: it's his house, not mine.

TARLETON. Who pays for it? Go and support yourself as I did if you want to be independent.

HYPATIA. I wanted to and you wouldnt let me. How can I support myself when I'm a prisoner?

TARLETON. Hold your tongue.

HYPATIA. Keep your temper.

PERCIVAL. (*coming between them*) Lord Summerhays: youll join me, I'm sure, in pointing out to both father and daughter that they have now reached that very common stage in family life at which anything but a blow would be an anti-climax. Do you seriously want to beat Patsy, Mr Tarleton?

TARLETON. Yes. I want to thrash the life out of her. If she doesnt get out of my reach, I'll do it. (*He sits down and grasps the writing table to restrain himself*).

HYPATIA. (*coolly going to him and leaning with her breast on his writing shoulders*) Oh, if you want to beat me just to relieve your feelings—just really and truly for the fun of it and the satisfaction of it, beat away. I dont grudge you that.

TARLETON. (*almost in hysterics*) I used to think that this sort of thing went on in other families but that it never could happen in ours. And now— (*He is broken with emotion, and continues lamentably*) I cant say the right thing. I cant do the right thing. I dont know what i s the right thing. I'm beaten; and she knows it. Summerhays: tell me what to do.

LORD SUMMERHAYS. When my council in Jinghiskahn reached the point of coming to blows, I used to adjourn the sitting. Let us postpone the discussion. What until Monday: we shall have Sunday to quiet down in. Believe me, I'm not making fun of you; but I think theres something in this young gentleman's advice. Read something.

TARLETON. I'll read King Lear.

HYPATIA. Dont. I'm very sorry, dear.

TARLETON. Youre not. Youre laughing at me. Serve me right! Parents and children! No man should know his own child. No child should know its own father. Let the family be rooted out of civilization! Let the human race be brought up in institutions!

HYPATIA. Oh yes. How jolly! You and I might be friends then; and Joey could stay to dinner.

TARLETON. Let him stay to dinner. Let him stay to breakfast. Let him spend his life here. Dont you say I drove him out. Dont you say I drove y o u out.

PERCIVAL. I really have no right to inflict myself on you. Dropping in as I did—

TARLETON. Out of the sky. Ha! Dropping in. The new sport of aviation. You just see a nice house; drop in; scoop up the man's daughter; and off with you again.

BENTLEY *comes back, with his shoulders hanging as if he too had been exercised to the last pitch of fatigue. He is very sad. They stare at him as he gropes to* PERCIVAL'S *chair.*

BENTLEY. I'm sorry for making a fool of myself. I beg your pardon. Hypatia: I'm awfully sorry; but Ive made up my mind that I'll never marry. (*He sits down in deep depression*).

HYPATIA. (*running to him*) How nice of you, Bentley!

Of course you guessed I wanted to marry Joey. What did the Polish lady do to you?

BENTLEY. (*turning his head away*) I'd rather not speak of her, if you dont mind.

HYPATIA. Youve fallen in love with her. (*She laughs.*)

BENTLEY. It's beastly of you to laugh.

LORD SUMMERHAYS. You are not the first to fall today under the lash of that young lady's derision, Bentley.

LINA, *her cap on, and her goggles in her hand, comes impetuously through the inner door.*

LINA. (*on the steps*) Mr Percival: can we get that aeroplane started again? (*She comes down and runs to the pavilion door*) I must get out of this into the air: right up into the blue.

PERCIVAL. Impossible. The frame's twisted. The petrol has given out: thats what brought us down. And how can we get a clear run to start with among these woods?

LINA. (*swooping back through the middle of the pavilion*) We can straighten the frame. We can buy petrol at the Beacon. With a few laborers we can get her out on to the Portsmouth Road and start her along that.

TARLETON. (*rising*) But why do you want to leave us, Miss Szcz?

LINA. Old pal: this is a stuffy house. You seem to think of nothing but making love. All the conversation here is about love-making. All the pictures are about love-making. The eyes of all of you are sheep's eyes. You are steeped in it, soaked in it: the very texts on the walls of your bedrooms are the ones about love. It is disgusting. It is not healthy. Your women are kept idle and dressed up for no other purpose than to be made love to. I have not been here an hour; and already everybody makes love to me as if because I am a woman it were my profession to be made love to. First you, old pal. I forgave you because you were nice about your wife.

HYPATIA. Oh! oh! oh! Oh, papa!

LINA. Then you, Lord Summerhays, come to me; and all you have to say is to ask me not to mention that you made love to me in Vienna two years ago. I forgave you because I thought you were an ambassador; and all ambassadors make love and are very nice and useful to people who travel. Then this young gentleman. He is engaged to this young lady; but no matter for that: he makes love to me because I carry him off in my arms when he cries. All these I bore in silence. But now comes your Johnny and tells me I'm a ripping fine woman, and asks me to marry him. I, Lina Szczepanowska, MARRY him!!!!! I do not mind this boy: he is a child: he loves me: I should have to give him money and take care of him: that would be foolish, but honorable. I do not mind you, old pal: you are what you call an old—ouf? but you do not offer to buy me: you say until we are tired—until you are so happy that you dare not ask for more. That is foolish too, at your age; but it is an adventure: it is not dishonorable. I do not mind Lord Summerhays: it was in Vienna: they had been toasting him at a great banquet: he was not sober. That is bad for the health; but it is not dishonorable. But your Johnny! Oh, your Johnny! with his marriage. He will do the straight thing by me. He will give me a home, a position. He tells me I must know that my present position is not one for a nice woman. This to me, Lina Szczepanowska! I am an honest woman: I earn my living. I am a free woman: I live in my own house. I am a woman of the world: I have thousands of friends: every night crowds of people applaud me, delight in me, buy my picture, pay hard-earned money to see me. I am strong: I am skilful: I am brave: I am independent: I am unbought: I am all that a woman ought to be; and in my family there has not been a single drunkard for four generations. And this Englishman! this linendraper! he dares to ask me to come and live with him in this rrrrrabbit hutch, and take my bread from his hand, and ask him for pocket money, and wear soft clothes, and be his woman! his wife! Sooner than that, I would stoop to the lowest depths of my profession. I would stuff lions with food and pretend to tame them.

I would deceive honest people's eyes with conjuring tricks instead of real feats of strength and skill. I would be a clown and set bad examples of conduct to little children. I would sink yet lower and be an actress or an opera singer, imperilling my soul by the wicked lie of pretending to be somebody else. All this I would do sooner than take my bread from the hand of a man and make him the master of my body and soul. And so you may tell your Johnny to buy an Englishwoman: he shall not buy Lina Szczepanowska; and I will not stay in the house where such dishonor is offered me. Adieu. (*She turns precipiately to go, but is faced in the pavilion doorway by* JOHNNY, *who comes in slowly, his hands in his pockets, meditating deeply*).

JOHNNY. (*confidentially to* LINA) You wont mention our little conversation, Miss Shepanoska. It'll do no good; and I'd rather you didnt.

TARLETON. Weve just heard about it, Johnny.

JOHNNY. (*shortly, but without ill-temper*) Oh: is that so?

HYPATIA. The cat's out of the bag, Johnny, about everybody. They were all beforehand with you: papa, Lord Summerhays, Bentley and all. Dont you let them laugh at you.

JOHNNY. (*a grin slowly overspreading his countenance*) Well, theres no use my pretending to be surprised at y o u, Governor, is there? I hope you got it as hot as I did. Mind, Miss Shepanoska: it wasnt lost on me. I'm a thinking man. I kept my temper. Youll admit that.

LINA. (*frankly*) Oh yes. I do not quarrel. You are what is called a chump; but you are not a bad sort of chump.

JOHNNY. Thank you. Well, if a chump may have an opinion, I should put it at this. You make, I suppose, ten pounds a night off your own bat, Miss Lina?

LINA. (*scornfully*) Ten pounds a night! I have made ten pounds a minute.

JOHNNY. (*with increased respect.*) Have you indeed?

I didnt know: youll excuse my mistake, I hope. But the principle is the same. Now I trust you wont be offended at what I'm going to say; but Ive thought about this and watched it in daily experience; and you may take it from me that the moment a woman becomes pecuniarily independent, she gets hold of the wrong end of the stick in moral questions.

LINA. Indeed! And what do you conclude from that, Mister Johnny?

JOHNNY. Well, obviously, that independence for women is wrong and shouldnt be allowed. For their own good, you know. And for the good of morality in general. You agree with me, Lord Summerhays, dont you?

LORD SUMMERHAYS. It's a very moral moral, if I may so express myself.

MRS TARLETON *comes in softly through the inner door.*

MRS TARLETON. Dont make too much noise. The lad's asleep.

TARLETON. Chickabiddy: we have some news for you.

JOHNNY. (*apprehensively*) Now theres no need, you know, Governor, to worry mother with everything that passes.

MRS TARLETON. (*coming to* TARLETON) Whats been going on? Dont you hold anything back from me, John. What have you been doing?

TARLETON. Patsy isnt going to marry Bentley.

MRS TARLETON. Of course not. Is that your great news? I never believed she'd marry him.

TARLETON. Theres something else. Mr Percival here—

MRS TARLETON. (*to* PERCIVAL) Are y o u going to marry Patsy?

PERCIVAL. (*diplomatically*) Patsy is going to marry me, with your permission.

MRS TARLETON. Oh, she has my permission: she ought to have been married long ago.

HYPATIA. Mother!

TARLETON. Miss Lina here, though she has been so short a time with us, has inspired a good deal of attachment in—I may say in almost all of us. Therefore I hope she'll stay to dinner, and not insist in flying away in that aeroplane.

PERCIVAL. You must stay, Miss Szczepanowska. I cant go up again this evening.

LINA. Ive seen you work it. Do you think I require any help? And Bentley shall come with me as a passenger.

BENTLEY. (*terrified*) Go up in an aeroplane! I darent.

LINA. You must learn to dare.

BENTLEY. (*pale but heroic*) All right. I'll come.

LORD SUMMER- | No, no, Bentley, impossible. I
HAYS. | shall not allow it.
MRS TARLETON. | Do you want to kill the child? He
| shant go.

BENTLEY. I will. I'll lie down and yell until you let me go. I'm not a coward. I wont be a coward.

LORD SUMMERHAYS. Miss Szczepanowska: my son is very dear to me. I implore you to wait until tomorrow morning.

LINA. There may be a storm tomorrow. And I'll go: storm or no storm. I must risk my life tomorrow.

BENTLEY. I hope there will be a storm.

LINA. (*grasping his arm*) You are trembling.

BENTLEY. Yes: it's terror, sheer terror. I can hardly see. I can hardly stand. But I'll go with you.

LINA. (*slapping him on the back and knocking a ghastly white smile into his face*) You shall. I like you, my boy. We go tomorrow, together.

BENTLEY. Yes: together: tomorrow.

TARLETON. Well, sufficient unto the day is the evil thereof. Read the old book.

MRS TARLETON. Is there anything else?

TARLETON. Well, I—er (*He addresses* LINA, *and stops*) I—er (*He addresses* LORD SUMMERHAYS, *and stops*) I —er (*He gives it up*) Well, I suppose—er—I suppose theres nothing more to be said.

HYPATIA (*fervently*) Thank goodness!

You Shouldn't Have Told
ANNE THOMPSON-SCRETCHING

*Winner of the 1997 Jean Dalrymple Award
for Best New Playwright*
"Cyclonic.... A sometimes hilarious, often searing
portrait of black urban America in the 1990s."
—*New York Post*

Standing-room-only audiences cheered the New York production
of this emotionally charged drama about a middle-class black family coping with a shameful tragedy. This is the story of a decent
mother who refuses to believe her three daughters when they tell
her that her boyfriend is sexually molesting them until the youngest dies from a botched abortion. It touches a nerve that crosses
class and cultural experiences. 4 m., 5 f. (#27610)

Mr. Bundy
JANE MARTIN

"Jane Martin has written her strongest play yet."
—*Theatrescope*

This powerful drama examines the fears of parents driven to do
"the right thing" to protect their daughter. Mom and dad learn that
their neighbor is a convicted child molester and consider both vigilance and vigilantism before being forced into action by a pair of
child advocacy crusaders. The shocking climax hits a nerve, leaving the audience to consider where the line between right and
wrong lies. This play was a hit at the 1998 Actors Theatre of Louisville Humana Festival. 3m., 1f., 1 f. child. (#15295)

Samuel French, Inc.
SERVING THE THEATRICAL COMMUNITY SINCE 1830

Other Publications for Your Interest

NOISES OFF
(LITTLE THEATRE—FARCE)

By MICHAEL FRAYN

5 men, 4 women—2 Interiors

This wonderful Broadway smash hit is "a farce about farce, taking the clichés of the genre and shaking them inventively through a series of kaleidoscopic patterns. Never missing a trick, it has as its first act a pastiche of traditional farce; as its second, a contemporary variant on the formula; as its third, an elaborate undermining of it. The play opens with a touring company dress-rehearsing 'Nothing On', a conventional farce. Mixing mockery and homage, Frayn heaps into this play-within-a-play a hilarious melee of stock characters and situations. Caricatures—cheery char, outraged wife and squeaky blonde—stampede in and out of doors. Voices rise and trousers fall . . . a farce that makes you think as well as laugh."—London Times Literary Supplement. ". . . as side-splitting a farce as I have seen. Ever? *Ever.*"—John Simon, NY Magazine. "The term 'hilarious' must have been coined in the expectation that something on the order of this farce-within-a-farce would eventually come along to justify it."—N.Y. Daily News. "Pure fun."—N.Y. Post. "A joyous and loving reminder that the theatre really does go on, even when the show falls apart."—N.Y. Times.   (#16052)

THE REAL THING
(ADVANCED GROUPS—COMEDY)

By TOM STOPPARD

4 men, 3 women—Various settings

The effervescent Mr. Stoppard has never been more intellectually—and *emotionally*—engaging than in this "backstage" comedy about a famous playwright named Henry Boot whose second wife, played on Broadway to great acclaim by Glenn Close (who won the Tony Award), is trying to merge "worthy causes" (generally a euphemism for left-wing politics) with her art as an actress. She has met a "political prisoner" named Brodie who has been jailed for radical thuggery, and who has written an inept play about how property is theft, about how the State stifles the Rights of The Individual, etc., etc., etc. Henry's wife wants him to make the play work theatrically, which he does after much soul-searching. Eventually, though, he is able to convince his wife that Brodie is emphatically *not* a victim of political repression. He is, in fact, a *thug*. Famed British actor Jeremy Irons triumphed in the Broadway production (Tony Award), which was directed to perfection by none other than Mike Nichols (Tony Award). "So densely and entertainingly packed with wit, ideas and feelings that one visit just won't do . . . Tom Stoppard's most moving play and the most bracing play anyone has written about love and marriage in years."—N.Y. Times. "Shimmering, dazzling theatre, a play of uncommon wit and intelligence which not only thoroughly delights but challenges and illuminates our lives."—WCBS-TV. 1984 Tony Award-Best Play.   (#941)

Other Publications for Your Interest

THE OCTETTE BRIDGE CLUB
(LITTLE THEATRE—COMIC DRAMA)

By P.J. BARRY

1 man, 8 women—Interior

There are no less than *eight wonderful roles for women* in this delightful sentimental comedy about American life in the 30's and 40's. On alternate Friday evenings, eight sisters meet to play bridge, gossip and generally entertain themselves. They are a group portrait right out of Norman Rockwell America. The first act takes place in 1934; the second act, ten years later, during a Hallowe'en costume/bridge party. Each sister acts out her character, climaxing with the youngest sister's hilarious belly dance as Salome. She, whom we have perceived in the first act as being somewhat emotionally distraught, has just gotten out of a sanitarium, and has realized that she must cut the bonds that have tied her to her smothering family and strike out on her own. This wonderful look at an American family in an era far more innocent and naive than our own was quite a standout at the Actors Theatre of Louisville Humana Festival of New American Plays. The play did not succeed with Broadway's jaded critics (which these days just may be a mark in its favor); but we truly believe it is a perfect play for Everybody Else; particularly, community theatres with hordes of good actresses clamoring for roles. "One of the most charming plays to come to the stage this season . . . a delightful, funny, moving glimpse of the sort of lives we are all familiar with—our own."—NY Daily News "Counterpunch".   (#17056)

BIG MAGGIE
(LITTLE THEATRE—DRAMA)

By JOHN B. KEANE

5 men, 6 women—Exterior/Interior

We are very proud to be making available for U.S. production the most popular play by one of contemporary Ireland's most beloved playwrights. The title character is the domineering mother of four wayward, grown-up children, each determined to go his own way, as Youth will do—and each likely headed in the wrong direction. Maggie has been burdened with a bibulous, womanizing husband. Now that he has died, though, she is free to exercise some control over the lives of herself and her family, much to the consternation of her children. Wonderful character parts abound in this tightly-constructed audience-pleaser, none finer than the role of Maggie—a gem of a part for a middle-aged actress! "The feminist awareness that informs the play gives it an intriguing texture, as we watch it unfold against a colorfully detailed background of contemporary rural Ireland. It is at times like hearing Ibsen with an Irish brogue."—WWD.   (#4637)

A WEEKEND NEAR MADISON

(LITTLE THEATRE—COMIC DRAMA)

By KATHLEEN TOLAN

2 men, 3 women—Interior

This recent hit from the famed Actors Theatre of Louisville, a terrific ensemble play about male-female relationships in the 80's, was praised by *Newsweek* as "warm, vital, glowing . . . full of wise ironies and unsentimental hopes". The story concerns a weekend reunion of old college friends now in their early thirties. The occasion is the visit of Vanessa, the queen bee of the group, who is now the leader of a lesbian/feminist rock band. Vanessa arrives at the home of an old friend who is now a psychiatrist hand in hand with her naif-like lover, who also plays in the band. Also on hand are the psychiatrist's wife, a novelist suffering from writer's block; and his brother, who was once Vanessa's lover and who still loves her. In the course of the weekend, Vanessa reveals that she and her lover desperately want to have a child—and she tries to persuade her former male lover to father it, not understanding that he might have some feelings about the whole thing. *Time Magazine* heard "the unmistakable cry of an infant hit . . . Playwright Tolan's work radiates promise and achievement." (#25051)

PASTORALE

(LITTLE THEATRE—COMEDY)

By DEBORAH EISENBERG

3 men, 4 women—Interior
(plus 1 or 2 bit parts and 3 optional extras)

"Deborah Eisenberg is one of the freshest and funniest voices in some seasons."—*Newsweek*. Somewhere out in the country Melanie has rented a house and in the living room she, her friend Rachel who came for a weekend but forgets to leave, and their school friend Steve (all in their mid-20s) spend nearly a year meandering through a mental landscape including such concerns as phobias, friendship, work, sex, slovenliness and epistemology. Other people happen by: Steve's young girlfriend Celia, the virtuous and annoying Edie, a man who Melanie has picked up in a bar, and a couple who appear during an intense conversation and observe the sofa is on fire. The lives of the three friends inevitably proceed and eventually draw them, the better prepared perhaps by their months on the sofa, in separate directions. "The most original, funniest new comic voice to be heard in New York theater since Beth Henley's 'Crimes of the Heart.'"—N.Y. Times. "A very funny, stylish comedy."—The New Yorker. "Wacky charm and wayward wit."—New York Magazine. "Delightful."—N.Y. Post. "Uproarious . . . the play is a world unto itself, and it spins."—N.Y. Sunday Times. (#18016)

Racing Demon
DAVID HARE

"Riveting."
NEW YORK MAGAZINE

"David Hare ... can shake a soul."
TIME MAGAZINE

This award-winning play premiered at the Royal National Theatre and at Lincoln Center. Attracting unwanted publicity, the Church of England is racked with dissention over matters of doctrine and practice and is at odds with the government. Reverend Lionel Espy and his team of clery struggle within this volatile climate to make sense of their mission in South London. Winner of four prestigious "Best Play" awards. 8 m., 3 f. (#19956)

Sacrilege
DIANE SHAFFER

"A play charged with genuine ideas."
WCBS TELEVISION

·"Compelling. SACRILEGE moved me to tears."
VARIETY

Ellen Burstyn starred on Broadway in this riveting drama about a devout Catholic nun who is fighting the Vatican to allow women in the priesthood. Her evenutal expulsion from her order forces others to re-examine the meaning of faith, spiritual violence and the redeeming grace of God. 6 m., 3 f. (#20977)

Samuel French, Inc.
SERVING THE THEATRICAL COMMUNITY SINCE 1830

Other Publications for Your Interest

TALKING WITH . . .
(LITTLE THEATRE)
By JANE MARTIN

11 women—Bare stage

Here, at last, is the collection of eleven extraordinary monologues for eleven actresses which had them on their feet cheering at the famed Actors Theatre of Louisville—audiences, critics and, yes, even jaded theatre professionals. The mysteriously pseudonymous Jane Martin is truly a "find", a new writer with a wonderfully idiosyncratic style, whose characters alternately amuse, move and frighten us always, however, speaking to us from the depths of their souls. The characters include a baton twirler who has found God through twirling; a fundamentalist snake handler, an ex-rodeo rider crowded out of the life she has cherished by men in 3-piece suits who want her to dress up "like Minnie damn Mouse in a tutu"; an actress willing to go to any length to get a job; and an old woman who claims she once saw a man with "cerebral walrus" walk into a McDonald's and be healed by a Big Mac. "Eleven female monologues, of which half a dozen verge on brilliance."—London Guardian. "Whoever (Jane Martin) is, she's a writer with an original imagination."—Village Voice. "With Jane Martin, the monologue has taken on a new poetic form, intensive in its method and revelatory in its impact."—Philadelphia Inquirer. "A dramatist with an original voice . . . (these are) tales about enthusiasms that become obsessions, eccentric confessionals that levitate with religious symbolism and gladsome humor."—N.Y. Times. *Talking With* . . . is the 1982 winner of the American Theatre Critics Association Award for Best Regional Play.   (#22009)

HAROLD AND MAUDE
(ADVANCED GROUPS—COMEDY)
By COLIN HIGGINS

9 men, 8 women—Various settings

Yes: *the Harold and Maude!* This is a stage adaptation of the wonderful movie about the suicidal 19 year-old boy who finally learns how to truly *live* when he meets up with that delightfully whacky octogenarian, Maude. Harold is the proverbial Poor Little Rich Kid. His alienation has caused him to attempt suicide several times, though these attempts are more cries for attention than actual attempts. His peculiar attachment to Maude, whom he meets at a funeral (a mutual passion), is what saves him—and what captivates us. This new stage version, a hit in France directed by the internationally-renowned Jean-Louis Barrault, will certainly delight both afficionados of the film and new-comers to the story. "Offbeat upbeat comedy."—Christian Science Monitor.   (#10032)